IT IS
ABOUT
LEADERSHIP...
NOT JUST
MANAGEMENT

IT IS
ABOUT
LEADERSHIP...
NOT JUST
MANAGEMENT

This book provides practical insights to help you develop authenticity, inspire your team, and lead with purpose. Discover how to go beyond mere management and become the leader others want to follow.

RANDALL DOIZAKI

Doizaki on Leadership LLC

8601 W. Cross Dr. F5 #138

Littleton, CO 80123

https://www.doizakionleadershipllc.com

Paperback ISBN - 979-8-9916910-0-0

Book Cover Design and Interior Formatting by 100Covers.

Printed in the USA

The information presented in this publication represents the view of the author as of the date of publication. This book is presented for informational purposes only. Due to the rate of changing conditions and the constant development of leadership training, the author reserves the right to alter and update his opinions based on new conditions. While every attempt has been made to verify the information in this book, neither the author or his affiliates/partners assume any responsibility for errors, inaccuracies, or similarity to other content. This book is a culmination of over 40 years of personal leadership experience of the author.

This book is dedicated to my wonderful wife, and patient daughter for all the years they have supported my journey towards self-improvement. They are the unwavering foundation of our family. Your impact on my journey is immeasurable.

Table Of Contents

II

III

What They Say About Randall

Randall, is able to speak to us on an operational level and works with us to solve problems.

Randall has an outstanding work ethic and is a visionary, his thinking and applications always encompass the entire project and involves all of the team respectfully.

Randall is a proven leader in everything he does. His compassion and integrity never sways, and his loyalty is beyond reproach. Along with his great work ethic comes a wildly fun sense of humor!

With such a wonderful demeanor and work ethic, Randy is definitely someone that I look up to and look forward to continuing to work with in the years to come.

Relates well with everyone.

He shows a sense of humor, is easily approachable, and takes pride in his job.

He is loyal, straight-forward, and easy to get along with. He is a team player, supports others, and has a good sense of humor.

He does a good job of helping to solve problems.

Has deeply ingrained beliefs towards conviction and follow through.

Is always open to new ideas and is willing to listen.

Has good tactical knowledge to offer in situations of conflict.

Has high expectations and encourages team members to excel whether in the department or personal.

Preface

In my role as an adjunct college faculty member, I emphasized that effective management encompasses the aspects of planning, organizing, leading, and controlling (POLC). Leadership manifests itself not only in formal roles but also in communities, churches, sports, and our families. I always try to emphasize that one can exhibit leadership without a title, but successful management requires a strong foundation in leadership.

Reflecting on my career transition from the Marine Corps to law enforcement going from patrol to investigations and subsequent promotions to sergeant and eventually lieutenant, a valuable piece of advice stayed with me: "Remember where you came from." This principle is my motivation for writing today. I aim to look back and reflect on my diverse responsibilities and interactions throughout the years, shaping the leader I am today. I intend for this reflection to serve as a valuable tool to support others on their leadership journey. Given the rapidly evolving landscape of technology and societal interactions, it is crucial to identify and mentor future leaders.

The pressing question remains, "**What proactive steps are we taking today to cultivate the leaders of tomorrow?**"

As a leader, it is imperative to know when to step aside and allow others to take the lead. To facilitate this transition, we need to guide and develop individuals in planning for the future today, rather than deferring it until the last moment.

My extensive experience, spanning over forty years, in various supervisory roles across different sectors has been based on this work.

It builds a foundation that guides the essence of "simple LEADERSHIP" from front-line operations to the executives of any organization. This is not an academic or statistical analysis of corporations. Instead, it offers practical, down-to-earth applications of fundamental principles that everyone can relate to. You may even recognize aspects of your own actions and behaviors in the scenarios described within this book.

This book is part of a broader succession plan, crafted to guide those embarking on their careers towards a promising start and to challenge seasoned leaders to step beyond their comfort zones. As you read through these pages, take time to reflect on how these insights resonate with you and those you influence. Embrace the journey of learning, growing, and sharing these insights with others.

Randall

Personal Reflection

1. Identify someone who was a formal or informal mentor to you at any time in your life, it can be more than 1 person.

2. Identify a LEADER/Manager you have worked for that you enjoyed working for and why.

3. Identify a LEADER/Manager you did not enjoy working for and why.

4. List characteristics you expect in a LEADER and/or manager and what you feel is the difference.

5. Identify someone you have worked with on their OWN personal/professional growth and why them. It can be more than 1 person.

"Ain't No Use Looking Down, Ain't No Answer on the Ground"

I know "Ain't" is not a proper word in the English language but it fits well in calling cadence (for marching) in the military and I thought it was appropriate to use with a coworker who I observed so deep in thought that she was missing what was going on around her.

I was walking by the employee entrance of the building we both work in and stopped to open the door for her. She was so buried in thought while looking more at her feet and where she was stepping that she did not see me holding the door until she went to open it. The thought came to me about a cadence in the Marine Corps (a clean one to use in this case) that went "Ain't no use looking down, ain't no discharge on the ground."

I took this and changed the word "discharge" for "answer" and then in discussion with the coworker I told her "Ain't no use looking down, ain't no answer on the ground." At first, she seemed puzzled by my comment, but when I mentioned about her being so deep in thought that she did not see me, she stated she did have a lot on her mind.

With a little discussion she shook her head and said she understood my comment and headed off to her office for the day. I had the opportunity to mention this to some other coworkers later in the day and some got a laugh out of it while others seemed just as puzzled by the concept. I have even noticed the CEO of the organization doing the same thing as he walks down the hall, being so deep in thought that he is looking down and missing what is going on around him sometimes.

This is not to say we miss everything, just that we need to look up, or as another phrase states, seeing the forest for the trees. As a second level supervisor/ mid-level manager in our organization I get directions from my supervisors and must pass them along to line staff, sometimes the operations seem overwhelming and we walk around looking down.

Often is the time we all take a break away from our desk or the pressure of the daily grind with the economy, family, work and try to fit time in with our support team. My wife is the greatest but it is not often that we have time to look up at what is going on even with our wonderful daughter. We are usually running out the door for work, school or coming in the door and getting ready for the next day. Even if we do get a "date night" in we must force ourselves to look up.

How many of our coworkers, friends and family spend the time looking down and not at what is going on around them?

A week later I had the opportunity to talk to the coworker that I had first mentioned this to. She told me she had caught herself looking down even when taking the dogs for a walk. She went on to say that it has made a difference in her mental attitude with a simple conscious effort of looking up, because there ain't no answer on the ground.

I stopped one day and watched our daughter and her friends come running out of the classroom while she was in elementary school. They were all looking up, not just for their parents but also to see what was going on around them. If we only take the time to look at things with a child's eyes, we might enjoy what we see a lot more.

I hope I can be the kind of parent that my daughter will learn from to include; there "Ain't no use looking down, ain't no answer on the ground."

I

Evaluate the Manner You Project Yourself

Reflect on how you present yourself. When we reminisce about those who came before us in our lives, we recall unique memories associated with them. At gatherings or retirement parties, conversations often revolve around amusing incidents from our past.

These memories, though amusing, stand out because they reflect our daily interactions or distinctive aspects of a person's character. As we reflect on our own journey through life, we tend not to recall the initial times we learned basic skills like tying our shoes or feeding ourselves. Rather, we move forward with the sum of all of our experiences shaping our character into who we are today.

The habits we develop today shapes our future and beyond. For an example, I began tucking my boot laces into my boots during my time in the Marine Corps, a habit I continued as a law enforcement officer to prevent them from snagging on obstacles during operations.

Consider seemingly mundane habits like the order you put on your socks or shoes, or where you place your coffee cup on your desk. These routines stem from our personal histories, making us creatures of habit. Reflect on the origins of your habits and how they influence others' perceptions of you. Consider how you will be remembered based on these habitual behaviors.

Even minor actions, such as sitting up and projecting a positive attitude when answering a phone call, can affect the image we convey to others. In customer service, a simple smile while answering the phone can be heard and appreciated, it changes your mindset, sharing a positive call. Similarly, think about your posture during a call—whether you are leaning back or leaning forward—a reflection of your engagement and seriousness about the conversation.

With today's technology enabling constant communication, how you handle your phone during conversations matters. Do you put it down and give your full attention to the person you are speaking to, or do you allow distractions? Consider the message you convey through your use of instant communication based on the situation and the person involved.

Personal Notes

Be Willing to Take a Different Path

Be prepared to blaze a fresh path through the jungle, as the current one might seem convenient but could be fraught with hidden obstacles.

I recall a memorable experience from a training session I attended several years ago. The speaker began by inquiring how many of us present had children. After a pause, about six out of approximately fifty attendees raised their hands.

The speaker proceeded to ask how many of us raised our hands to reply to a blind person. He had entered with a cane, and the materials indicated his visual impairment.

My point is that we consider the pattern of behavior on how we react out of habit. This instinctive reaction is a technique commonly utilized in the military and law enforcement as a survival mechanism. It is also fundamental in martial arts training. While it is valuable in various circumstances and can be essential when applied appropriately, if it turns into a routine, it may lead to complacency and predictable patterns.

In military and law enforcement, relying on routine paths can have negative effects on us and those around us. During jungle training in the military or neighborhood patrols, we often stick to well-taken paths or established routines. This may expedite our journey or ensure we cover critical areas during our shifts. However, it could also expose us to potential traps along the usual route or cause us to overlook something on a less-traveled street because others can predict our habits and patterns. Avoid being predictable in all cases, but not in personal relationships.

Take this beyond mere muscle memory, even in seemingly simple actions like changing a roll of toilet paper—does it unroll from the top or the bottom? Is this a conscious, deliberate act or just a routine replacement? It might seem insignificant, but the issue lies in whether you make a conscious effort to replace it the same way every time.

The point is not about the toilet paper direction, but about your willingness to consider a new path and exhibit distinct leadership. Try switching seats at a meeting or training session and observe people's reactions. How many times have you encountered the phrase, "We've always done it that way"?

We need to pause and question why. Have you ever taken a moment to question why we do what we do and if we can do it better? If so, how, and what could the potential outcomes be?

Over time, we form routines and habits, becoming predictable. Even our team members learn how to approach us or how to trigger certain reactions. How open are you to stepping beyond your comfort zone and taking a less traveled path? When did you last challenge something that did not align with what needed to be done?

However, change should not be for the sake of change. From a leadership perspective, few things are more challenging than a "manager" introducing a change without considering the ripple effect on operations or the rest of the team. Change just for change's sake is disruptive and, honestly, disrespectful of the team's time and resources. When considering the change, involving the team, and gaining their support will significantly increase the likelihood of its success.

Square Your Gig Line – Are You in Alignment?

Align your mission: maintain precision and readiness by frequently checking your alignment with your goals.

Do your actions align with your mission, personally and professionally? In a uniform, the gig line is a straight line running from the shirt seam down the belt buckle edge to the pants zipper, in perfect precision.

In critical situations, who do we turn to? Often, it's call in the Marines or the Police, their image projecting a sense of can-do and readiness. As a Marine (once a Marine, always a Marine) and retired lieutenant in law enforcement, I understand the importance of taking charge in challenging situations. While others may run, we step forward, running towards the threat, showing our resolve and preparedness.

I encourage you to evaluate your own "gig line" — your alignment and precision. Do you keep it as straight as a Marine in uniform? How do you stay sharp and aligned? What sets the Marine Corps apart from other branches? It is about attitude, unity, and pride — the Esprit De Corps that defines us.

In my experience as an evidence sergeant, I emphasized attention to detail, ensuring the little things were handled correctly, making the big things routine. "WYA" or "Watch Your Assets" emphasizes proactive action over reactive explanations. Keeping your "gig line" straight, both literally and metaphorically, simplifies explanations later.

In law enforcement, being proactive and maintaining alignment with our mission is crucial. It is about confidently watching our assets going in, ensuring we do our best based on the available information. This proactive approach builds a solid attitude, setting an example for those we lead.

As a leader, being proactive means continually evaluating our approach, embracing industry trends, training our team, and developing our skills. It is about protecting our assets — our people and our reputation. So, how square is your gig line? Will you stand up when called upon, or wait for someone else to act? It's about being aligned and ready, maintaining the precision and readiness of a well-kept gig line.

How Does Your Uniform Fit?

As a Marine or Police officer, the impact of one's appearance and posture cannot be overstated. When you walk into a room in uniform, you carry more than just the weight of your gear; you carry an image, a statement of who you are and the dedication you have to your profession.

People take notice of how you present yourself—the neatness of your uniform, the shine of your shoes, and the overall attention to detail. But it is not just about looking sharp; it is about projecting confidence, authority, and respect.

Every button meticulously secured, every crease sharp, and every shoe shining with your reflection; these details matter. They are not just about adhering to a dress code or a set of regulations; they reflect the discipline and attention to detail that is instilled in a Marine or a Police officer. It is a daily reminder that excellence is not an exception—it is the standard.

I recall a challenging moment during a uniform inspection in the Marine Corps. After the inspecting officer looked me over and poked at a few things on my duty belt, he noticed a loose thread on a button of my well-pressed shirt. He then proceeded to pull on the thread, causing the button to come off.

While it might seem trivial to some, his insistence on perfection left a lasting impression. I had to resew every button on the shirt to include having the threads all running in the same direction. It reminded me that in our profession, even the smallest details can make a significant difference.

That loose thread was a metaphor for the potential weaknesses that can unravel the fabric of our professionalism if left unattended.

In law enforcement and the military, we are not only judged by our actions but also by our appearance. The way we look in our uniform can influence how the community perceives us. When we respond to a call and show up with impeccable grooming and posture, we show command presence. Conversely, a dirty and messy appearance, like wearing your lunch on your shirt, can undermine your authority and impact effective communication.

A Marine striding into a room in Dress Blues exemplifies this impact. The straight back, the head held high, and the meticulously maintained uniform all send a powerful message of pride, discipline, and dedication. It sets a standard for others to aspire to and shows a sense of honor and duty.

It is essential to recognize that the expectations for appearance may vary in different environments. As a Marine, retired law enforcement professional, adjunct college faculty, and leadership consultant, I have experienced this firsthand. In the academic setting, projecting a professional image through business attire elevates the level of respect and expectation from students. It sets a tone for the learning environment and communicates a sense of seriousness and dedication.

However, regardless of the setting, the principle remains the same: how we present ourselves matters. It affects not only how others perceive us but also how we perceive ourselves and the standards we uphold.

Beyond appearance, posture plays a critical role in conveying confidence and authority. When a Marine or Police officer walks into a room with a straight back and a confident stride, it communicates readiness and strength. It is a non-verbal cue that speaks volumes about the individual's mindset and level of preparedness.

Conversely, a slouched posture or an unconfident gait can undermine authority and convey doubt. It is crucial to be aware of our body language and use it to our advantage, projecting the image of a competent and capable professional.

In the military, law enforcement, or any profession, appearance and posture are not superficial matters. They are reflections of our dedication, discipline, and commitment to excellence. It is about recognizing the power of perception and understanding that how we present ourselves directly influences how we are perceived and, consequently, how effective we can be in our roles.

As you get ready everyday for work and you put on your uniform or work clothes, take a moment to reflect on the power it holds—not just as a piece of clothing, but as a symbol of your identity and the ideals you represent. Let it remind you of the standards you have sworn to uphold, the discipline you have embraced, and the impact you can make by presenting yourself with pride and professionalism.

Ensure Thorough Knowledge of Your Tools

While the need for an in-depth understanding of a rifle may not directly translate to the private sector, the fundamental principle of mastering the skills required to respond swiftly to any situation remains universal. This can be compared to the rigorous training routines seen in martial arts or the meticulous routines in gymnastics, ballet, and other sports. In the corporate world, it equates to understanding your role and responsibilities thoroughly, preparing for unexpected challenges, and being adaptable.

In the military and law enforcement, the emphasis on attention to detail extends beyond operational duties. Careful maintenance of gear and frequent inspections is a routine that helps maintain readiness and uphold standards. This discipline is comparable to the need for attention to detail and thorough preparation in the business realm. In the corporate world, this is shown as meticulous planning, regular review of strategies and resources, and adhering to industry best practices to ensure smooth operations and optimal performance.

The practice of paying attention to appearance and being well-prepared is similar to the military tradition of meticulously polishing boots and maintaining a sharp uniform. While not literally about uniform appearance in the private sector, the principle extends to presenting oneself in a professional and presentable manner. It is about the perception you create, demonstrating that you hold yourself to high standards and take your role seriously.

Leadership in both law enforcement and the military involve setting a high standard, often demonstrated through actions, routines, and adherence to protocols. Similarly, in the corporate world, effective leadership entails setting an example, establishing clear expectations, and maintaining a culture of discipline and professionalism. The idea is to inspire and motivate teams to perform at their best and align with the organization's goals and values.

In essence, the lessons from military and law enforcement experiences can be translated into the private sector by focusing on preparation, attention to detail, presenting a professional image, and embodying strong leadership qualities. These principles are timeless and can significantly contribute to success and effectiveness across different professional domains.

Maintain Your Focus — Are You on Track, and Can You Sustain It?

In the military and law enforcement professions, maintaining focus and precision in aiming and shooting is a critical skill. After discharging a round from the rifle or handgun, rigorous drills are conducted to swiftly realign and repeatedly hit the target accurately. This practice mirrors the need for agility and adaptability in rapidly changing environments. Similarly, in the private sector, businesses must swiftly realign their strategies and approaches to hit their targets effectively, especially in dynamic market conditions.

You can apply this same approach to organizing your week. In the military, planning the week involves defining major objectives and prioritizing them. The tasks that demand immediate attention are placed at the forefront. Likewise, in the private sector, effective weekly planning involves setting key goals and organizing tasks in order of priority. Tackling the most critical objectives first is a common practice in both military operations and business operations.

When given an objective or establishing a goal, having a clear vision of the end goal is crucial across all sectors. This is a shared principle in the military, law enforcement, and the private sector. In the military, a clear objective is essential for a successful mission. In law enforcement, defining the goal of an investigation or operation guides the team. Similarly, in the private sector, a company sets a clear objective to guide its strategies and actions.

In a college course, working with students on academic papers involves a structured process. This structured approach, which includes research, organizing information, and drafting the paper, has parallels in how the military plans and executes operations. Just as in the military, where detailed planning and preparation are vital for a successful mission, a well-organized approach is crucial in academic and professional endeavors.

Many of us have participated in meetings that are conducted out of routine or habit. Conducting a meeting without an agenda is a waste of time, a sentiment that resonates across the military, law enforcement, and the private sector. In these sectors, efficiency and productivity are highly valued, and having a clear agenda ensures that meetings are purposeful and provide actionable outcomes.

To reach a successful outcome, it is important to go beyond the basic questions of how, who, what, when, where or why, and truly understand the objective at hand. This approach is ingrained in the military and law enforcement, where understanding the mission's core purpose is crucial. Likewise, in the private sector, businesses should aim to thoroughly understand the objective they are striving for, ensuring all efforts align with the overarching goals.

While keeping the above in mind, do not overlook the "big picture." In fact, let us substitute the term "details" with "Sight picture" in this scenario. In the military, law enforcement, and the private sector, focusing on the "big picture" is essential for overall success. It allows for a strategic view of goals, not getting bogged down in minor details, which is vital in decision-making and resource allocation.

In summary, principles of focus, strategic planning, clear goal-setting, structured processes, efficient meetings, and understanding the "big picture" are fundamental across the military, law enforcement, and the private sector. These shared principles highlight the interconnectedness and transferability of leadership and organizational skills across diverse professional domains.

Personal Notes

The Title Is Earned, Never Given

Earning the title "United States Marine" is a profound achievement, an accomplishment of the rigorous dedication and discipline required in the military. This journey has parallel standing with law enforcement profession and the private sector, where each domain demands a unique approach to earning respect and achieving excellence.

In the military, the demanding process of training and transformation during boot camp serves as a crucible (a term used in all military branches). It molds individuals into a cohesive unit, instilling core values such as honor, courage, and commitment. Similarly, in law enforcement, the rigorous training at academies cultivates discipline, ethical conduct, and the ability to make split-second decisions under pressure.

Transitioning to the private sector, parallels can be drawn in the pursuit of professional growth and success. Much like in the military and law enforcement, where advancement is achieved through merit and competency, the corporate world values expertise, dedication, and results. Climbing the corporate ladder involves proving one's capabilities and demonstrating leadership qualities in the pursuit of organizational goals.

However, each domain manifests distinct organizational cultures and leadership styles. The military and law enforcement often emphasize hierarchical structures and a clear chain of command to maintain order and ensure coordinated actions. In contrast, the private sector may adopt more decentralized approaches, fostering innovation, adaptability, and employee empowerment.

Respecting titles and earned roles are a common principle across all three domains. Wearing the uniform, badge, or title represents a level of expertise and experience that commands respect and acknowledgment. It is essential to uphold the responsibilities and expectations associated with a title, whether it is "Marine," "officer," or a corporate leadership position.

Understanding the unique demands and dynamics of each sector is crucial for successful transition or collaboration. The transferable skills of discipline, adaptability, teamwork, and problem-solving gleaned from the military and law enforcement can be invaluable assets in the corporate world, enriching organizations and contributing to a diverse and capable workforce.

Assist a Fellow Marine With Their Uniform – We're Stronger Together

Reflecting on teamwork, a vivid memory from boot camp comes to mind—preparing for inspection alongside others in my platoon. As a unit, we helped one another get our inspection uniforms on, meticulously ensuring perfection, no detail overlooked. It was a collective effort, from pulling up trousers to tucking in shirts, to checking for stray fibers.

Who has been there to aid you with your uniform? Or whom have you supported recently with theirs?

In my roles as a first and second level supervisor in law enforcement, we conducted quarterly uniform and equipment inspections. These inspections evaluated not only staff appearance and uniform condition but also served to ensure accountability for issued equipment, maintaining a sense of order and precision among everyone.

In both military and law enforcement, attention to detail and adherence to uniform and equipment standards are essential. The discipline and precision instilled during military service often finds a parallel in law enforcement, where a sharp, professional appearance is not just a matter of pride but a symbol of authority and discipline. These aspects are similarly critical in the private sector, albeit often less structured.

Another instance of this collaborative spirit occurs when submitting a progress report or research project. Having another set of eyes for review is crucial. As a leader, I often seek feedback from peers and subordinates, valuing insights regardless of their position. This practice not only ensures alignment but also sparks discussions that might impact operations beyond my initial considerations.

This process of review and feedback is like the debriefing sessions common in the military and law enforcement. After a mission or operation, a thorough review is conducted to identify what worked, what did not, and how to improve. The same principle applies in the private sector, where project post-mortems are conducted to analyze successes and failures, aiming to enhance future performances.

Consider the boost to team morale. By involving a broad spectrum of individuals in projects, we elevate their worth and add to their knowledge. Much like the military rank structure, preparing each rank to seamlessly step into higher roles showcases the foundation of succession planning. A business's failure to nurture and educate the next person in line can lead to operational breakdowns. Identifying and mentoring individuals for future positions is essential to ensure continuity of operations.

In the military and law enforcement, succession planning is deeply ingrained. Potential leaders are identified early, groomed, and given increasing responsibilities to prepare them for higher positions. This practice is not as standardized in the private sector, where companies often grapple with effective succession planning, potentially impacting the organization's stability and growth.

Yet, this process can inadvertently bruise egos and impact morale, both for the leader and those being led. Acknowledging our shortcomings, especially when someone else excels, can be challenging. Conversely, some individuals within the ranks might feel overlooked, believing they deserve a chance.

It is vital to maintain an ongoing dialogue between supervisors and the work group, emphasizing future leaders and establishing performance standards. This approach not only helps with the identification of potential leaders but also sets clear expectations for those not meeting the mark. Who knows, by taking a stance on their future, you might ignite a spark of interest and motivation in someone.

The military, law enforcement, and the private sector share fundamental principles of teamwork, attention to detail, accountability, and succession planning. Recognizing these similarities and adapting best practices from each sector can contribute to the overall growth and success of any organization, fostering a culture of collaboration, excellence, and continuous improvement.

Sleep Alongside Your Troops in the Trenches—Avoid Resting on High Ground if Your Troops Are Bedding Down in the Mud

I remember a lieutenant in our infantry unit (Lt. B.). When he joined the platoon, he would spend the entire day climbing hills with us and then set up his own shelter half. A shelter half is essentially half of a two-part tent that connects with another half carried by a different Marine, hence the name shelter half. Each Marine carries the tie-down cords and stakes for their portion of the tent.

This lieutenant would set up with the unit in the same area. After arranging his shelter half, he would begin working out, doing pushups. For most people, this would be the last thing on their minds. I mean, after a grueling day of nonstop movement and sweating profusely, most of us just wanted to sit back and catch our breath for a few minutes.

In the military, especially in infantry units, camaraderie and leading by example are essential. The lieutenant embodied this spirit by physically engaging in the same challenges as his troops, showcasing resilience and fortitude. This principle translates to the law enforcement profession, where officers often face demanding physical and mental challenges. A leader who can stand shoulder to shoulder with their team, sharing their burdens and demonstrating unwavering commitment, fosters a sense of unity and trust.

The underlying idea here is the example he set for his troops; he exceeded the basic expectations. He not only set the example, but he did it alongside the troops, without placing himself above the rest of us. Let us pause and reflect on the "perks" leaders may enjoy, from more spacious office areas to sometimes better hours and obviously higher pay.

In both the military and law enforcement, a leader's actions and dedication speak louder than titles or privileges. The mentioned "perks" are also visible in the private sector, where hierarchical structures can sometimes create a disconnect between leadership and the rest of the team. However, effective leaders, regardless of the sector, remember that their position is a responsibility and an opportunity to serve and inspire, not a pedestal for personal gain.

This is not to disregard that greater responsibility and duty deserve compensation. We are compensated for our knowledge and level of accountability. What is crucial is considering the shift in attitude when someone does attain that corner office. We need to remember our roots and the colleagues we have worked with in the trenches.

In all these domains, from the military to law enforcement and the private sector, a leader's journey begins with frontline experiences. The lessons learned while "in the trenches" are invaluable. The transition to a leadership role should never mean disconnection from the realities faced by the team.

A simple personal example of this for me is the shadow box on my desk in our home office. In this shadow box is the badge I proudly wore for over ten years as a sergeant with the Sheriff's Office. This badge was so outdated that they had even changed the pattern and words on it. Below the badge in the shadow box is the word "REMEMBER."

This serves as a reminder of those I served as a leader in the organization and the duty I have to them. I would not be the leader I am today without the work done by the team. After all, we cannot lead a team on our own; it requires a committed group effort.

How often do we have meals with the troops or invite them to the office for a cup of coffee? When was the last time you aided line staff with their work? Have you ever called someone to your office and had them sit in YOUR chair to have a conversation?

Never ask one of your team members to do something you are not willing to do. Good leaders never consider themselves above emptying the garbage or operating a piece of equipment if they are capable. It is an excellent way to earn respect and support the team.

Connect with the team – unwind with your team and colleagues.

In the military, camaraderie often revolves around shared challenges and a bit of friendly competition, frequently involving alcohol. However, these gatherings can sometimes lead to trouble. Similarly, in law enforcement, officers often develop strong bonds through shared experiences, but there is a fine line between camaraderie and unprofessional behavior.

In the private sector, the dynamics are different but equally important. While the context might not involve life-or-death situations, building a cohesive team is essential. The challenge is finding ways to foster social interactions that strengthen bonds without getting into inappropriate interactions.

Creating an open and approachable leadership style is critical in all three settings. In the military, approachable leaders can be the difference between a successful mission and a failure. Similarly, in law enforcement, officers need leaders they can trust and turn to for guidance.

In the private sector, approachability is often associated with effective leadership. Employees who feel comfortable approaching their supervisors with challenges, are more likely to voice concerns, leading to better problem-solving and a healthier work environment. The ability to relate to employees, regardless of the setting, can significantly impact team dynamics.

The importance of open dialogue is a common thread across these sectors. In the military, effective communication can save lives and ensure mission success. In law enforcement, it's crucial for coordinating efforts and addressing challenges.

In the private sector, open dialogue can lead to innovation and the sharing of valuable insights. Leaders who actively engage in discussions with their teams can uncover hidden talents and new perspectives, which can drive business growth.

In both the military and law enforcement, building personal connections and showing empathy is vital. Soldiers and officers often face high-stress situations and personal challenges. Leaders who take the time to understand their team members' lives outside of work demonstrate genuine care and concern.

Similarly, in the private sector, understanding the personal lives and challenges of employees can lead to a more supportive work environment. Leaders who show empathy and help when appropriate can improve job satisfaction and overall productivity.

In all sectors, finding the right balance between professionalism and personal connection is essential. While social gatherings and bonding activities can be beneficial, leaders must set clear boundaries to maintain a respectful and appropriate work environment.

All areas of leadership, the military, law enforcement, and the private sector have distinct challenges and contexts, there are common themes of leadership, communication, and empathy that apply across all settings. Learning from the experiences in each sector can help leaders become more effective in building and managing successful teams.

Maintain Silence During Patrol –
Awareness Requires Quiet

In both my experiences as a lieutenant in law enforcement and as a unit leader in the military, the value of silence and attentiveness during operations is critical. It is interesting how this principle applies similarly in the private sector, particularly in business, highlighting the cross-sectional importance of awareness and discretion.

In military patrols, maintaining silence is fundamental to ensure stealth, prevent revealing one's position, and gain a tactical advantage. Likewise, in law enforcement, especially during apprehensions or investigations, the element of surprise can be crucial for success. Similarly, in the business world, maintaining confidentiality during strategic moves or negotiations is vital to prevent competitors from gaining an advantage.

The military operates on a 'need-to-know' basis to restrict information access only to those who require it. Law enforcement follows similar protocols to ensure sensitive data is not leaked. Similarly, in business, restricting access to critical strategies or trade secrets to select personnel is a common practice to safeguard the company's interests and competitive edge.

In the military, being acutely aware of one's surroundings is essential for survival and mission success. Law enforcement professionals adopt a similar approach, continuously monitoring their environment for signs of potential threats. In the business world, being aware of market trends, competitor strategies, and customer preferences is pivotal to make informed decisions and stay ahead in the market.

The military often faces unpredictable and rapidly changing situations, necessitating adaptability and quick decision-making. Law enforcement encounters similar dynamics, requiring officers to adjust tactics swiftly. In the business world, agility and adaptability are equally crucial to respond effectively to market shifts, customer demands, or unexpected challenges.

In the military and law enforcement, clear and concise communication can mean the difference between success and failure. In the business world, it is vital for aligning teams, conveying strategic visions, and achieving organizational goals.

Military and law enforcement roles often involve hierarchical structures and a clear chain of command. Similarly, businesses have hierarchical setups with defined roles and authority. Effective leadership, delegation, and guidance are crucial in all sectors to ensure smooth operations and achieve objectives.

Drawing these comparisons emphasizes the extent of certain fundamental principles—silence and attentiveness, secure information handling, operational awareness, adaptability, effective communication, and solid leadership—that transcend specific professions and are foundational for success across various domains.

Personal Notes

Utilize the Radio Efficiently for Effective Communication in the Cp—Maintain Brevity and Clarity

Effective communication is a critical part of success in various domains—be it the military, law enforcement, or the private sector. In each arena, the ability to convey critical information swiftly and clearly is pivotal. Let us look at the parallels and distinctions between these different professional areas regarding communication strategies.

In the military, efficient radio communication utilizing the phonetic alphabet is a norm. Messages need to be brief, precise, and quickly comprehensible. This principle applies in law enforcement as well, where brevity and clarity over the radio are crucial for operational success.

In the private sector, particularly during business meetings, the essence of succinctness remains. However, the means of communication may differ, with the focus often shifting to key presentations and engaging speeches. The common thread remains the need for a clear and concise message.

In the private sector, while there may not be a universally adopted phonetic alphabet, there is a reliance on industry-specific acronyms and terms. These terminologies are similar to the phonetic alphabet, being specific to the profession and facilitating effective intra-industry communication.

In the military and law enforcement, visualization of roles and a clear understanding of everyone's function within an operation are paramount. Communication must convey these roles effectively to ensure a coordinated effort.

Similarly, in the private sector, especially during large-scale projects, the understanding of each team's role is vital. Communication, both in terms of instructions and progress updates, must be clear and targeted, aligning with the overall project objectives.

In law enforcement and the military, professionals are adept at adjusting their communication to suit diverse audiences, ensuring effective understanding across the board. This adaptability is a crucial aspect of their training.

In the private sector, particularly in client-facing roles, a similar adaptability is essential. Tailoring communication to suit the audience, avoiding jargon that might confuse, and explaining concepts in plain language are essential skills.

In the private sector, especially in boardrooms and meetings, there is a delicate balance between presenting data and maintaining clarity. A presentation of too much data can overwhelm the audience, leading to ineffective communication.

This mirrors situations in the military and law enforcement where excessive information can lead to confusion and hinder effective decision-making. Thus, the focus on presenting key points and relevant information is consistent across these domains.

Leaving a lasting impression involves concisely delivering the core message, reiterating the key points, and perhaps illustrating the message through engaging stories. This approach is vital in both the fast-paced and high-stakes environments of the military and law enforcement, as well as the competitive and dynamic landscape of the private sector.

In essence, the fundamentals of effective communication—brevity, clarity, audience adaptation, and a focus on core objectives—form a common thread across the military, law enforcement, and the private sector. Understanding and applying these principles within the unique contexts of each domain is fundamental to achieving success and desired outcomes.

Field Day the Barracks Together

Incorporating the military, law enforcement profession, and the private sector into the context of field day activities at the barracks provides valuable insights into their distinct operational dynamics and how teamwork is cultivated in each domain.

In the military, especially during barracks inspections, there is a stringent emphasis on discipline, precision, and adherence to established protocols. The structured hierarchy and chain of command dictate roles and responsibilities, ensuring a clear understanding of tasks. Teamwork is a fundamental aspect, where each member's contribution, no matter how seemingly small, is vital to the overall unit's efficiency. The military approach ingrains discipline, unity, and a sense of collective purpose, just like a well-coordinated mission.

In law enforcement, like the military, a disciplined and structured approach is essential. The focus on attention to detail, organization, and thoroughness aligns with the military's values. Inspections and collective duties in law enforcement emphasize maintaining a professional and orderly environment, reflecting the image of the force to the community. The coordination and collaboration required in law enforcement operations mirror the teamwork emphasized in the military, although with distinct objectives and strategies related to maintaining public safety and enforcing the law.

In the private sector, particularly in corporate settings, teamwork is also essential for achieving organizational goals. However, the nature of teamwork may differ. While the military and law enforcement operate within hierarchical structures, the private sector often adopts a more flexible and collaborative approach. Teams are cross-functional, requiring diverse skill sets and perspectives to solve complex problems. The dynamics are more fluid, and innovation and adaptability are encouraged. Moreover, the focus is not only on the task at hand but also on long-term organizational success and profitability.

Drawing comparisons between these sectors identifies the necessity of teamwork in various professional settings. Despite differing structures and objectives, the core principles of cooperation, collaboration, and understanding each team member's role remain consistent.

The military and law enforcement instill discipline and a strong sense of duty, while the private sector emphasizes innovation and adaptability, highlighting the diverse ways in which teamwork is fostered to achieve distinct organizational objectives.

Evaluate Readiness: Do Employees Have the Right Tools for the Job?

As part of our routine assessments, we ensured that our personnel had all the necessary gear, clothing, and field equipment in optimal condition. This encompassed thorough inspections of our uniforms, right from the cover (often referred to as a "hat" for civilians) down to our underwear. We paid attention to details like the spacing between hangers in the lockers or the arrangement of items on the bed, following a set display pattern.

This meticulous approach served two purposes: to uphold accountability and to foster a culture of structure and consistency in maintaining our gear. Surprisingly, even the simple act of pressing our underwear with an iron (minus the starch) was part of this regimen. We maintained a distinct set of uniforms and equipment exclusively for these inspections.

Drawing a parallel to the corporate environment, we can analyze the tools (or equipment/materials) provided that staff need to carry out their designated responsibilities. While ironing underwear may not align with typical workplace expectations, it does provoke reflection. Sometimes, even the most basic items can significantly impact employee dedication. By ensuring that staff have access to the tools they need, we empower them to channel their energy towards their duties and assignments.

The inspections in the military and law enforcement serve the purpose of accountability. Maintaining gear in top condition is not just about appearance but signifies an individual's commitment to their role and the organization. It also establishes a structured routine, reinforcing the importance of adherence to standards and consistency in performance.

Keeping a separate set of gear specifically for inspections emphasizes the significance of being well-prepared. It also implies the need to present a professional image and maintain a high standard of readiness for duty.

In the business world, readiness translates to having the appropriate tools, resources, and knowledge to perform job responsibilities effectively. Just like the military and law enforcement prepare their gear, businesses need to equip their employees with the necessary tools and resources required for their roles.

Consider how military and law enforcement personnel's commitment is enhanced through well-maintained gear, employees in the private sector feel valued and committed when provided with the tools they need to excel. It allows them to focus their energy on their tasks and responsibilities without unnecessary hindrances.

While the specifics may differ, the underlying principle remains the same - readiness and dedication are nurtured through adequate preparation and provision of the necessary tools and resources. This, in turn, translates to improved performance, accountability, and a strong sense of commitment among employees across various domains.

Develop and Support Small Teams

Building and fortifying the fire team - compact, robust, and diversified tactical groups - stands as a cornerstone in the military, law enforcement, and the private sector. In each of these domains, these teams serve critical functions and share fundamental principles.

In the military, from the smallest tactical units to the largest divisions, the importance of well-structured teams cannot be overstated. These teams are finely tuned and operate on the bedrock of clear and specific assignments for each member. This organizational model is echoed in law enforcement agencies, where patrol units, investigative teams, and special task forces each have their defined roles and functions.

The business sector mirrors this approach through project teams, departmental units, and cross-functional groups. Much like in the military and law enforcement, understanding the distinct roles and responsibilities of team members is crucial for success. The ability to comprehend and respect each other's expertise within the team ensures cohesive operations, fostering a unified front to face challenges.

Moreover, the necessity for backup and understanding one another's assignments is equally vital across all three domains. Whether it's the military, law enforcement, or the private sector, individuals can be unavailable due to various reasons, such as illness or unexpected circumstances. In such scenarios, a seamless transition, and the ability to temporarily cover for absent team members are indispensable.

This adaptability to fill in for one another in these high-stakes professions, be it in a combat situation, a criminal investigation, or a business project, can often be a make-or-break factor. It highlights the importance of not only having a solid team structure but also ensuring that each team member understands the broader objectives and is ready to support others when needed.

In conclusion, while the context and specifics may vary, the fundamental principles of team dynamics, role clarity, and mutual support are universal in the military, law enforcement, and the private sector. These principles underscore the essence of effective teamwork and collaboration, enabling successful mission accomplishment and organizational achievement.

Be Willing to Kick Them in the Assets….
(Figuratively, Not Physically)

In the military and law enforcement, the concept of discipline is ingrained deeply. The necessity to follow orders, adhere to strict protocols, and maintain a strong chain of command is vital for the effectiveness and safety of both organizations. This discipline cultivates a sense of structure and obedience, which can be paralleled in certain hierarchical structures within the private sector. For example, in corporations, clear reporting hierarchies and adherence to policies and guidelines are crucial for organizational efficiency and achieving collective goals.

Leadership in these domains is often characterized by a direct and assertive style. Decisions are made quickly and decisively, and leadership expects prompt execution of orders. This aligns with scenarios in the private sector, especially in industries with a fast-paced and dynamic environment, where quick decision-making and implementation are essential for staying competitive.

However, the approach to motivation can differ. In the military and law enforcement, motivation often stems from a sense of duty, honor, and commitment to a greater cause, such as protecting one's country or community. This contrasts with the private sector, where motivation frequently ties to personal and organizational success, financial incentives, career growth, and job satisfaction. Understanding and adapting to these varying motivational factors is crucial for effective leadership in each context.

In terms of accountability and performance evaluation, the military, law enforcement, and private sector each have their own frameworks. The military and law enforcement often have strict systems for assessing performance and conduct, with clear consequences for subpar performance. Similarly, the private sector employs performance evaluations and feedback mechanisms, although the evaluation criteria and consequences may differ. Effectively managing performance and addressing shortcomings is vital for success in any of these domains.

Lastly, communication is a fundamental aspect that ties these sectors together. Effective communication is critical in all areas, ensuring that objectives are understood, expectations are clear, and information flows smoothly within the organization. However, the styles and channels of communication may vary. The military and law enforcement often rely on direct, formal communication, while the private sector may embrace a mix of formal and informal channels, adapting to the culture and structure of each organization.

By recognizing these similarities and differences, leaders can better navigate and succeed in diverse environments, integrating the best practices from each domain to enhance their leadership capabilities.

Identify a Platoon Scribe… We All Need to Know Who Has What Responsibility

Developing a designated platoon scribe is essential for ensuring effective communication and efficiency within the unit. This individual plays a crucial role in handling tasks that require a particular skill set, ultimately keeping the unit on course. It is vital for every team member to know who to approach for support in various areas to prevent any operational setbacks. Failure to clearly communicate these responsibilities can lead to unit failure and hinder progress.

Drawing parallels between military, law enforcement, and the private sector underscores the significance of a designated role like a platoon scribe in various organizational settings. In the military, the concept of a platoon scribe aligns with the importance of precise documentation and communication. Military operations rely heavily on accurate records, from mission plans to after-action reports. A designated scribe ensures that crucial details are documented, aiding in decision-making, learning from past operations, and maintaining accountability.

Similarly, in law enforcement, effective communication and meticulous documentation are paramount. Police officers frequently deal with complex cases and legal procedures where accurate records are vital for investigations and court proceedings. A designated scribe in this context ensures that critical information related to cases, suspects, and evidence is recorded accurately, contributing to the integrity and effectiveness of law enforcement operations.

In the private sector, especially within corporate settings, the role of a designated scribe may not be as formally defined as in the military or law enforcement. However, the need for precise documentation and effective communication identifying who is responsible for what task is equally crucial. Whether it is in project management, strategic planning, or client interactions, accurate record-keeping identified duty assignments and transparent communication are vital for achieving organizational goals. Assigning someone the responsibility of a scribe ensures that important meetings, decisions, and strategies are documented, aiding in continuity and informed decision-making.

This arrangement not only benefits the unit in the present but also prepares others to seamlessly take over when necessary. I recall a conversation with a supervisor about my strengths and weaknesses during preparation for a promotion assessment. The supervisor emphasized the importance of clear task parameters when assigning duties. Providing guidance and setting expectations is crucial to prevent failure, wasted effort, and time.

In a significant project I was assigned, the supervisor emphasized a specific format for the presentation and report without providing clear instructions. This communication failure caused conflict and a program delay. Consequently, executive staff mandated a crash course for line supervisors in process planning due to the missed deadline.

As leaders, it is our responsibility to equip staff with the means to meet expectations and offer constructive feedback on their performance. Developing a platoon scribe, similar to a secretary taking meeting notes or project manager being assigned, is a way to ensure that vital information is accurately recorded and easily accessible. Additionally, having a designated go-to person for questions is a crucial consideration, ensuring that there is a reliable source of accurate information for future reference. If we neglect to establish a platoon scribe and maintain clear communication channels, we risk wasting valuable time and effort.

In summary, the role of a designated scribe, though formalized to varying degrees in different contexts, holds immense value across military, law enforcement, and private sector settings. The need for accurate documentation and effective communication remains a common thread, underlining the importance of a designated individual responsible for record-keeping and facilitating seamless operations. Understanding and implementing such practices can significantly contribute to the success and efficiency of any organization.

II

Bearing

In the military, bearing is a fundamental aspect of discipline and professionalism. Marines are trained to maintain a strong bearing, displaying confidence, alertness, and respect at all times. This includes maintaining a proper posture, alertness during drills, and respectful interactions with superiors, peers, and subordinates.

In the corporate world, bearing translates to maintaining a professional demeanor. A strong and confident posture, active engagement during meetings, and respectful communication with colleagues are all part of this. Imagine a business executive entering a meeting with confidence and addressing the team assertively. It conveys a sense of leadership and professionalism.

A military officer, standing tall and confident during a briefing, demonstrates bearing just as a CEO does when presenting in a boardroom.

Courage

Courage is a cornerstone of military training. It is about facing the unknown, enduring difficult conditions, and confronting fear. This can manifest in physical courage during combat or mental courage when making tough decisions under pressure.

In the workplace, courage can mean standing up for what is right, even when it is not the popular choice. It might involve taking calculated risks in business decisions or speaking out against unethical practices. For example, a business leader may need to confront a problematic issue within the company and make tough calls to address it.

A Marine displaying bravery in the face of danger mirrors a manager making a tough call to restructure a failing project.

Decisiveness

In the military, split-second decisions can be a matter of life and death. Training emphasizes the importance of making quick, informed decisions based on available information, even in high-stress situations.

Similarly, in business, decisiveness is crucial. A leader needs to make timely decisions, balancing available information and the urgency of the situation. For instance, a CEO may need to make a rapid decision on a new product launch based on market trends and consumer demand.

A military leader swiftly deciding the troop's course of action in battle is akin to a business leader making quick decisions during a crisis.

Dependability

Dependability is a military core value. Marines must be reliable in fulfilling duties, whether it's showing up on time for duty or completing tasks within specified deadlines.

In a civilian setting, dependability means showing up on time for meetings, meeting project deadlines, and fulfilling commitments to clients or colleagues. For instance, a project manager needs to ensure the team delivers on time to meet client expectations.

A Marine consistently showing up on time for duty is comparable to a team member consistently meeting project deadlines in an office setting.

Endurance

Endurance is honed through rigorous military training. It is about physical and mental resilience, pushing through challenges and fatigue, and still achieving the mission.

In a civilian context, endurance is essential for achieving long-term goals. It might mean working diligently toward a project deadline, staying committed to a fitness routine to achieve a health goal, or persisting through challenging times in a business venture.

A Marine enduring a long march in challenging conditions is like an entrepreneur persisting through tough times to make their startup successful.

Enthusiasm

In the military, enthusiasm is instilled through pride in one's unit and mission. It is about channeling that excitement and dedication into performance and teamwork.

In the workplace, enthusiasm can be infectious. A passionate and engaged team leader motivates their team, boosting morale and productivity. For example, a startup founder's enthusiasm for their product can inspire their team to work tirelessly toward its success.

A Marine's enthusiasm during a mission is comparable to a team leader's excitement about a new project in a corporate environment.

Initiative

Taking the initiative is highly valued in the military. It is about proactively identifying tasks that need to be done and acting without always needing explicit instructions.

Similarly, in the professional world, taking initiative means being proactive, identifying problems, and suggesting solutions without waiting to be directed. An employee who takes the initiative might propose process improvements that streamline operations within their department.

A Marine taking the initiative to set up a defensive position is like an employee suggesting a new process to enhance efficiency at work.

Integrity

Integrity is the bedrock of military ethics. It is about doing what is right even when no one is watching, being honest and transparent, and upholding ethical standards.

In the business world, integrity means adhering to a strong moral and ethical code. It involves being honest in dealings with clients, partners, and employees. For instance, a business leader might turn down a lucrative but unethical business opportunity, choosing integrity over profit.

A Marine's honesty about an error is like a businessperson being transparent about a mistake in a financial report.

Judgement

Military personnel are trained to make sound judgments under pressure, weighing the risks and benefits of each decision. It is about making the best decision based on the available information.

In the corporate world, good judgment is vital. Leaders need to make informed decisions that benefit the organization. For instance, a project manager must assess the project's status and decide whether additional resources are needed to meet the deadline.

A military officer's decision-making process in a time-sensitive situation mirrors a manager's approach to addressing urgent matters in a company.

Justice

In the military, justice is about fair treatment and adherence to laws and regulations. It ensures all individuals are treated fairly and equitably.

In the business realm, justice is reflected in fair treatment of employees, equal opportunities for growth, and just resolution of conflicts. For example, a HR manager must ensure fair disciplinary actions and unbiased treatment of all employees.

A fair disciplinary action for a military offense is akin to just resolution of a dispute in the workplace.

Knowledge

Continuous learning is a military norm. Personnel are encouraged to stay updated on technology, tactics, and strategies to adapt to evolving threats.

In the professional world, continuous learning is essential for growth and innovation. Staying updated with industry trends, new technologies, and evolving best practices helps professionals excel in their careers. For instance, a marketing executive should continually learn about emerging digital marketing trends.

A Marine keeping up-to-date with the latest tactics is like a marketing executive staying informed about current trends in advertising.

Loyalty

Loyalty to the unit and fellow soldiers is a fundamental military value. It is about standing by your team, supporting them, and working together toward common goals.

In business, loyalty translates to supporting colleagues and the organization's mission. It is about showing commitment to the company's goals and values. For example, a sales team showing loyalty would support and uplift each other, ensuring collective success.

A Marine's loyalty to their unit is comparable to a team's loyalty to their company, supporting each other in achieving shared objectives.

Tact

Tact is vital in the military for effective communication and maintaining morale. It involves delivering messages with sensitivity and diplomacy.

In the corporate world, tactful communication is essential. It is about providing feedback, making suggestions, or addressing sensitive topics in a way that is considerate and respectful. For instance, a manager providing constructive criticism to a team member uses tact to maintain a positive working relationship.

A Marine using tactful communication with a distressed comrade resembles a manager using tact when giving constructive feedback to an employee.

Unselfishness

Unselfishness in the military means prioritizing the team over personal interests. It involves sacrificing personal comfort for the greater good of the unit.

In a civilian setting, unselfishness means putting the team or organization's interests ahead of personal gain. It might involve sharing credit for success with the team or supporting colleagues in achieving collective goals. For example, a team leader sharing credit with the team after a successful project showcases unselfishness.

A Marine sacrificing personal comfort for the team is like an employee putting in extra effort to help a team meet a deadline.

III

Random Thoughts and Points to Consider

- Beware the actions of others; question their motivation and ask if they are acting in the interest of the organization or for personal reasons.

- Pay close attention to the praise or interaction you have with others. As people, we tend to recognize those we associate with or those of like-mind. At times, this leads to more praise and interaction than we show others. A leader must be fair across the board. Find reasons to interact with others.

- To defend against a weapon, you do not need to be an expert with the weapon, you just need to know how it can be used. The same for leadership; you need to understand the obstacles in front of you and take the challenge to overcome them.

- We often give someone a "pat on the back" as a means of appreciation and recognition; people are social creatures and a little sincere recognition goes a long way. However, they may be wondering where the other hand is. Is it over their head waiting to hit them if they make a mistake?

- A shortcut is not always that easy, others may know about it as well. It just becomes an alternate route and may not be any quicker.

- Some can multi-task and others are just multi-thinkers. We are also seeing an increase in those with ADD or ADHD; this means they either must change the way their brain is wired or we change the way we interact with them. The first is not very likely, requiring us to change our approach as leaders

- Just like working with someone in a negotiation situation, we need to give them an out. Leave options open when dealing with others. If it becomes an all-or-nothing situation, it may end up being a lose/ lose situation.

- We often talk about how high up the chain someone may be. If we look at this like climbing a tree, the most influential sit higher. We need to cut down the tree and put everyone on the same level, just on different paths.

- The mountain rams can be heard for miles charging and hitting their curled horns against each other, trying to show their dominance. In the end, one wins and the other loses, just to come back and try again next year.

- Some seek a specific goal to be good. As leaders we need to push them to be great and then go beyond that level.

- As a leader, you need to ask how many will follow you into battle, even to the death, because of who you are and not just because of the title you have.

- Do the research on different types of leadership power (coercive, expert, legitimate, referent, or reward) and do a self-evaluation on which style you use.

- Can you list an adjective to describe yourself for each letter in the alphabet?

- Compare ROE (return on effort) to ROI (return on investment) as a leader and for the performance of those you work with.

- Sometimes it may be best to make a tactical withdrawal, back off, reassess, and redeploy. This may include just taking a walk and having some inactive activity. Just go watch the wind blow across the field.

- Just like taking a piece of coal under pressure over a period of time will give you a diamond, with some pressure and guidance that weak employee, with potential, may be your diamond. Hopefully, it will not take as long as nature does to make a diamond.

- Take a day and try not to use a microwave. Think about how our society interacted before microwaves and cell phones. Try to brush your teeth or to eat a meal with your weak hand.

- If people are so full of themselves, they have little room to think of new ideas or consider those they work with.

- Think about the first time asking someone out on a date or starting a new job. This same fear can be seen in those we work with on new projects or teams. Be patient and work through it with them.

- We are all in sales, even if we just do data entry. Think about selecting a brand of pasta off the store shelf. Even picking out the clothes from the closet to wear to work; we are selling ourselves. Our decisions may not be influenced by others, but we are still selling ourselves on the value of the item, by price, taste, fit, or appearance.

- I recall attending an open house recruiting event for an employer and how it looked like a school dance. All of the prospective candidates were sitting on one side of the room and the staff on the other. How do your functions look?

- We all have the ability to apply mind over matter. That is, it should not matter in our lives, unless someone puts a gun to our face or places our lives in danger, and then we should mind.

- Opportunity does not always knock on your door; opportunity may be waiting for you to knock. You need to be willing to go out and put yourself in the right place at the right time and knock on opportunity's door.

- Even a beehive, with all the swarming bees, has organized chaos. It may not always seem to be the same within an organization; we may need to step back and take a look from a distance.

- If I hold up a blank piece of paper between us, which side is the front? Does it matter which side you are looking at? Or do I get to say, since I am holding up the paper?

- In every branch of the military, we call cadence while running to keep everyone in step. However, we also develop our lungs from the forced breathing. It may seem futile, but the benefits are great.

- Even a simple journeyman knows which tool to use on which job. In leadership, we occasionally try to use a hammer when a screwdriver would work better. Know your tools and when to use them.

- Have you ever been out to dinner with someone you were trying to impress; a friend, a boss, a client, and then spilled your food? Sometimes it becomes a problem when we focus so hard on doing things right that we make a mistake. We may need to just let some things play out without trying to manipulate them.

- Some see the fruit, others the color, and yet others see the spelling of the word if you ask them to think of orange. Think about how your message is received and the intended audience.

- If you are driving down the highway and you keep looking over your shoulder to see what has already passed, you end up driving off the road or running into something else.

- Even the master at Bonsai knows it will take years of careful trimming and pruning to bring out the character of the plant that he sees.

- In studies of officer-involved shootings or military strategy, we find the foundation of perception of the situation, processing of the situation, and reaction to the situation. This occurs in an instant, yet in leadership we often miss some of the first or even second parts and react without properly perceiving the situation or processing it.

- Just like putting on a mask at Halloween, we have different costumes for different occasions. We need to question if we are true to the real person. I ask new officers if they make the badge or if the badge makes them. Part of this is to get them to understand that people will respect the person behind the badge.

- The first point in boot camp is to break down the person and mold them into a Marine, based on years of service from those that have gone before. Think about those who have gone before in your organization and their legacy.

- Looking at a child learning to walk or tie their shoes, we have to wonder how we have stumbled along and how those we work with will grow into future leaders.

- An approachable leader hears a little of everything and can put together the bigger picture of the overall unit morale. This helps prevent issues from being a surprise later.

- Big words do not make a person bigger.

- Remember that on occasion you may need to KYOC (keep your own counsel).

- When rappelling (using a rope to lower yourself down a mountain), you need to have someone you trust working the line to keep you steady.

- Our military never shows the palm of their hand when saluting; this is a sign of surrender. Think about how you project yourself; do you show you have surrendered without even thinking about it?

- When we have police call in the military (picking up trash in the area) all staff assist. This means everyone is on the same level.

- We constantly work on eliminating the "ME, MY, I" attitude and to develop the "US" in the unit.

- Practice projecting your voice, like calling a cadence while marching, or when talking softly to someone in distress. You need to be able to monitor how your message may be received.

- Research and read material outside of your normal area of interest. Get out of your comfort zone.

- It is an honor to lead others and it becomes an essential duty to assist them.

- Look out for the "TEAM" and all of the "TEAM MEMBERS."

- Network upfront not after the fact; connect from day one, inside and outside.

- Do not stand for mediocrity or average when you know they can do better.

- Know when to manage and when to lead. Sometimes you need to give others room to make a mistake to learn. But, with other situations, you may need to step in and give specific orders. The trick is to know when.

- If you want to be popular, do not be a leader. Respect is earned, never taken. Having a title will not automatically make others respect you; often they end up fearing the power you have over them.

- Challenge issues/ topics as a champion and as a devil's advocate. You must be willing to say what is not pleasant, even to those who supervise you.

- Shut down rumors and do not allow them to run amok. These can often create a division among staff, even when the information is not true.

Twenty-five Questions

1. What is your favorite field of study (whether your own specialty or another) and why?

2. What or who got you started in this field of study?

3. What do you feel are the 3 most important characteristics or personality traits for someone in your specialty?

4. How do you feel when you know you will have to talk to others or teach others about your work (nervous, excited, how do you prepare, etc.)?

5. How do you explain your interest to your friends/ family/ peers?

6. What impact does your chosen field of interest have on your family/friends?

7. What three pieces of advice would you give to someone interested in this field of study?

8. How do you feel about the image or perception of this area of interest?

9. Has this perception had any effect on what you tell people when asked what you do for a living/ hobby?

10. How far ahead have you planned for your own retirement?

11. What will you do when you retire?

12. How do you cope with the reality of what you see and know about humanity?

13. Where do you foresee your specialty headed over the next 10 years?

14. What is your most positive memorable experience in this area?

15. What is your most negative memorable experience in this area?

16. What are your favorite foods/favorite meal?

17. Do you play any sports?

18. What is the one thing you wish more people knew about you?

19. If you could go back in time, what period of time would you visit?

20. What is your dream vacation?

21. If you could live anywhere in the world, where would you live?

22. Dinner in or dinner out?

23. Do you have any pets?

24. Do you ask someone to record the news if you know you will be on?

25. Do you do any volunteer work?

Share these with the team and compare answers.

I Am a Bully…. Leadership Myth?

A few years ago, I presented a point of consideration to two different groups of employees (in law enforcement) that is that we may be perceived as bullies by the mere profession we work in and the authority we carry in our duties. If we look at the definition of a bully, we may agree that roughly a bully is:

A person who exerts control over another through a position of power by whatever means or authority to gain compliance and or/to influence/ intimidate the other person to do what we want.

This is not to say we set out to bully anyone, but if we look at any leadership position, anyone of us could be perceived to be a bully. That is, we influence others due to our position of authority over them. We as leaders/ managers have a direct impact on the current status or future opportunity for those we supervise. If we do not like them personally or how they perform their duties or even the manner that they address us, we have options to deal with them in a positive or negative manner.

Does this make us a bully, or more specifically we may be perceived as a bully because we intimidate them by our very position, which some carry as power over others.

How much of a shadow do we cast over them on mountain as a leader?

How often have we heard that we intimidate others or that we are not approachable because they fear what the outcome might be if others speak their mind. Think back in your own career path or previous jobs when you hesitated or even backed down from addressing an issue with someone else in your chain of command.

Why did you hesitate to speak your mind in a situation that could have had a different outcome or even not say anything at all?

In law enforcement, we are seen as the ultimate authorities on a scene, when we show up in uniform with the badge on, WE are exerting authority over others. The point of my discussion with those I work with is that we need to be aware of how others may perceive our presence and that they may automatically be defensive.

For the private sector or any leadership position, we need to step back and be willing to recognize that our directives or interaction with others may interfere with open communication. We need to encourage others to challenge ideas and that they need to look at different methods of achieving the end goal, we only get this by getting away from the attitude that we are better than them and by understanding that we may be seen as a bully, even if it is not openly discussed.

I recently meet with an employee on a performance issue to discuss how we could improve his performance and plan for his future. One of the points I made was that as a leader, I need to be looking for the future leaders in the organization and sometimes that requires pushing others to step up and perform better as well as holding them accountable for errors. This employee was very agitated and asked to speak openly about the issue; of course, I stated by all means tell me what is on his mind.

Well, this person stated that he did not trust me. We continued for a few moments when I asked why he did not trust me, the response was that I bully him. I shook my head and acknowledged his comment, without any alarm on my part.

He stepped back and stated "this doesn't concern you." I replied that I supervise over fifty employees and that I cannot please everyone and that I know I come across as a bully. I went on to say I am a strong personality, and as a Marine I have a big ego (law enforcement generally are type "A" personalities) and that I am responsible for all staff while on duty, and that I constantly challenge everyone on the team to do their best, yes, I AM A BULLY.

However, regardless of how I tried to explain to him that my intent is not to intimidate others, just to build strong individuals as decision makers and as members of a cohesive team, he just would not let go of the issue that I bully him.

So, the question I ask is, as leaders how do we address the mindset that we are bullies by the position/ title we hold?

In discussions with others, it came out that we can only go into it being aware of how we are perceived. We cannot change how others react to our instructions or leadership style; we can only be aware of their possible perceptions. This will aid us in developing others and with any succession plans. To address this with line staff we need to develop open dialogue and truly follow an open-door policy.

As the leader of staff in a profession with the most serious possible impact on others, this being the potential cost of life over others, we constantly challenge staff; and yes, this can come across as being a bully.

Later after talking with this employee, I sat down with other members of the team and discussed my leadership style. When asked about being a bully, some shook their head and said not in the least. Yet others stated they understand why I approach things the way I do and that they actually grow under the push to excel.

The bottom line is we cannot please everyone, we can only show good leadership and set the example of the standards we expect. Good luck in trying to make everyone happy; no matter how hard we try we may still be an unintentional bully.

Leaders Must Be Weak

As leaders in our respective fields, how often do we find ourselves standing outside of the work group looking in?

I have asked others in supervisory positions if they are supervisors or superiors to those they manage. Many answer quickly with either answer without giving it much thought. Once we dig into the question and clarify why they gave the answer they chose, it becomes clear that some of them put themselves above the line level.

This is not to say that they are poor leaders, just that their mind set has separated them from those doing the work. One of the major points I have found is that they see themselves as needing to be better or that they are above others. This creates a rift in the communication process and prevents others from feeling comfortable talking with them about any issues that may have negative consequences.

To work on this, we look at the perceived attitude that they can do no wrong and how they make the right choices all the time. But to be honest, we cannot say we never made a poor decision. I encourage those I work with to look at the poor choices made as opportunities and areas needing improvement, then we challenge them to build on those points.

Leaders must be weak and be willing to show that they are not all mighty.

A. Be approachable, not above the line level

Many of us at any supervisor level talk about having an open-door policy and that we are willing to hear from any and all in the organization. However, often those that use the open door are only those that have a complaint or feel that they have been treated unfairly by a person or policy standard. Yet, on the other hand, you may have those that are trying to self-promote by using the open door to keep themselves in the spot light.

So, to address this attitude among staff, we need to approach them in their work area. That is, we need to "manage by walking around", you cannot expect them to come to you if you are not willing to go see them. By opening the channel of communication with others it makes it easier for them to feel comfortable walking into your office. This also gives us some insight into the daily operations around us.

But for this to be effective, we need to "Talk less, listen more." Ask open-ended questions and solicit feedback on what is being done. Even if they or you have made a decision or planned a poor course of action, wait for their response, and take action later. Be willing to tell a story about past operations and how things have changed; give them some ideas on what was and what can be. Make a comment about operations or point something out to them about the work or area. Let them know you are paying attention.

B. Admit mistakes

How often do we address mistakes made by our direct reports?

How often do you admit your mistakes in front of others, not just to your supervisors?

I have often heard other supervisors, at all levels of the organization from line to executive level, start off a conversation about a mistake someone made with "what were you thinking, this is a mess and you need to get it cleaned up," or by showing someone where they made the mistake.

It has proven to be much more effective to start off by asking them to explain their thought process or steps taken in the situation that gave them the results you are looking at.

Then you need to ask the questions to get them to think about other options, it is all part of the learning process and builds them into future decision makers.

To build on this, we as supervisors need to acknowledge our errors to those we work with. If we are not willing to demonstrate we make mistakes and only speak of the great things we do, we are not setting an example for others to follow. It is much easier to have others come to us and let us know about something if they are comfortable and feel safe in knowing we will not take their head off.

We may even learn something from others by discussing our errors openly. Think about how much we have learned over the years by seeing, doing, and reviewing. But this has not been done by our own efforts, we interact with others on a daily basis and those interactions dictate how we proceed.

This includes asking for feedback both from those we answer to and those we supervise. We often know what to expect from those we answer to and how to prepare a presentation or idea to present to them. However, we generally forget to include those that may have to implement the idea or to ask them if it even makes sense to them. Think about how well it be supported if others can understand the concept and have some feedback on improving the idea, you will be halfway to getting the approval and buy-in.

C. Be willing to roll up their sleeves, or as in the military sense, sleep in the mud with the troops.

How often do you stop and offer to help someone with a project?

Looking back at my time in the Marine Corps, I recall a few officers who would sleep in the same area as the troops and other officers that would move off to the side from the unit. We had more respect for those that integrated with the unit. In law enforcement, I have always been one of those supervisors that participate in the training with the teams. This has included driving, firearms, arrest control (defensive tactics) and other classroom sessions. By being active with the team and going through the same training, staff can see that I have weak areas and strong areas; we all laugh and joke about the same issues.

In most organizations it is easy to see where a leader can step in and give a hand. This is not just about coaching or mentoring someone or working with them on a project. We also need to be willing to pick up the slack on occasion if they need us to. On different teams I would go into the briefing room before the team came on duty and place a small piece of paper towel on the floor at both ends of the room. Staff would have to walk past one or the other and most would leave it where it was. I would then point out how we all need to keep an eye on our work area and as a team pitch in. I would then pick up the piece of paper myself.

How does this help me to roll up my sleeves? By setting the example and not being above the team when it comes to pitching in, I am not any better than anyone else; I have weaknesses, I must admit my mistakes and I must be willing to pick something up off the floor.

Training or Conduct

In a recent conversation with others on staff management, we touched on disciplinary actions and improvement plans for poor performance It surprises me how many supervisors or managers fail to identify if the issue is TRAINING or CONDUCT related. In order to address the performance issue, we need to identify the root cause, did we fail the employee through poor training or does the employee just not care? If we cannot show adequate training was provided it falls on us. If the training meets the expectation and the employee failed to follow the training or policies, it is on the employee.

So, How Do You, as a Leader, Help?

Do you take the easy path? Why do we always look for the easy task? Why do some excel and others just coast through life? As LEADERS, we need to be willing to take on the tough challenges and seek out ways to help our teams learn and grow. As a LEADER, how have you challenged your team? Are you willing to take the path less traveled, or just follow in the footsteps of others? Remember; Managers direct and control others LEADERS encourage and develop others

Awards

Out of all the awards and department letters of recognition none of them mean anything compared to the thanks from an officer who just finished the academy and field training program. I do not even have my degree posted in my office or home; the accomplishments of the team mean more than a piece of paper.

Look around you and at your desk or office and ask what you have on display. Do you showcase your personal achievements, is that what others see about you?

As a leader what do you display or show about the team and their work?

Tired Old Dog

As a career public servant with years of experience and an education in leadership I have many conversations with the next generation of leaders and ask them where they want to be when I step aside. But I must wonder how many other "Leaders" take the time to identify future leaders to take over for them. Most of us never stop to consider what will be our legacy within the organization or even look for those with the spark to be an exceptional leader and decision maker for the future.

Troops Eat First

One of the issues that has come up over the years is about leaders eat last. Now I have an issue with this, not the concept, but the manner it is presented.

In all my years of service, the Marine Corps, law enforcement, school safety and even the private sector, we all try to emphasize troops first. And this is where the phrase leaders eat last came into play.

The issue I have with this is that we start off talking about the leader, when we should be starting off with the troops first. It is the mindset that we are talking about what leaders are or are not doing, when we should be focused on the troops.

So, I challenge you to change this around and that you use the idea that "Troops eat first" make it about them not the leader.

Challenge

So, I challenge all of you to consider these questions:

1. Who mentored you?

2. What would you have done differently in your own career to be a better LEADER?

3. How do you share the idea of "LEADERSHIP" and being a great LEADER?

4. Do you have a succession plan in place? Remember, Managers control and direct others LEADERS encourage and develop others And LEADERSHIP starts with LEADER

Prioritizing Wellness: A Leader's Guide to Fostering Resilience and Mental Health in High-Stress Professions

Introduction

In high-stress professions, the well-being of employees is critical. When employees carry the weight of their work home, it impacts not just their mental health but also their families. This newsletter focuses on the essential steps leaders must take to ensure their teams maintain a healthy state of mind and why prioritizing personal wellness is essential for organizational success.

The Impact of Workplace Leadership on Families

The actions and expectations of workplace leadership influence the families of our employees. It is critical to remember that the stress and emotional trauma from work often spills over into family life. One of the discussions I have with others in a coaching session and professional interactions is that we all need to have friends outside of our profession, we need to be able to leave work at work. Leaders should strive to create an environment where employees can leave work concerns at the door, encouraging a positive work-life balance that benefits both them and their families.

The Emotional Health of Our Employees

A positive workplace environment directly correlates with physical and emotional wellness, productivity, and retention. Leaders must be mindful of how their actions and decisions affect their team's morale and well-being. Ensuring fair treatment and avoiding actions that compound stress are key to maintaining a healthy, supportive atmosphere.

Confronting the "Tough Guy" Culture in High-Stress Professions

Many high-stress professions have long been steeped in a "tough guy" culture, where admitting stress or seeking help is often seen as a sign of weakness. This mindset can prevent employees from addressing their mental health needs, leading to burnout, decreased performance, and even severe psychological issues. Leaders must actively work to dismantle this stigma by promoting a culture of openness and support where employees feel safe to express their vulnerabilities without fear of judgment.

Employees need to know that acknowledging stress and seeking support is a sign of strength, not weakness. Leaders can set the tone by openly discussing their own challenges and how they manage stress, thereby normalizing the conversation around mental health.

Creating and Maintaining a Positive Organizational Culture

A culture that values employee well-being and promotes a positive work environment leads to greater effectiveness and job satisfaction. Leaders should know their team members on a personal level, showing genuine interest in their lives, which builds a supportive and cohesive community within the workplace.

Leadership Courage and Its Role in Employee Wellness

Effective leaders need the courage to address concerns directly and set clear, actionable expectations for their team. This involves providing open and honest feedback and ensuring that supervisors are equipped with the training and support they need to lead effectively. Consistent reinforcement of these expectations is necessary to sustaining a positive organizational culture.

The Need for Authentic Leadership in High-Stress Professions

Today, many high-stress professions face unprecedented challenges in retention and recruitment, often linked to low morale. Authentic leadership, rooted in strength and humility, can inspire, and motivate employees, fostering a sense of belonging and commitment. Leaders who embrace these qualities and demonstrate genuine care for their team can counteract the negative trends in the field.

Building Resilience in Employees

Resilience training is essential for equipping employees with the tools to handle stress and adversity. Programs that teach coping mechanisms, emotional intelligence, and stress management techniques can significantly enhance employees' ability to maintain a positive mindset and make sound decisions under pressure. Peer support and camaraderie also play a vital role in fostering resilience.

Holistic Wellness Programs for High-Stress Professions

Addressing the holistic wellness of employees involves focusing on physical, mental, and emotional health. Implementing comprehensive wellness programs that include fitness initiatives, mental health services, and support for work-life balance can greatly improve overall well-being. Leaders should advocate for resources and policies that promote these aspects of wellness.

Leadership and Organizational Support

Effective leadership and strong organizational support are critical in promoting employee wellness. By fostering a culture that prioritizes self-care and reduces the stigma around seeking help, leaders can create a supportive environment. Participation in wellness initiatives and open communication are key to maintaining high morale and job satisfaction.

Assessment Questions for Team Well-being

Leaders can use these five questions to assess their team's well-being and identify areas for improvement:

1. How often do team members express feeling stressed or overwhelmed at work? This helps gauge the overall stress level within the team and identify common stressors.

2. Do employees feel they have adequate support and resources to manage their workload? Understanding the perceived level of support can highlight gaps in resources or leadership.

3. How comfortable are team members in discussing their mental health or personal concerns with their supervisors? This question assesses the level of trust and openness within the team.

4. What aspects of their job do team members find most fulfilling or rewarding? Identifying these can help leaders focus on enhancing positive elements that boost morale.

5. How do employees feel about the balance between their work responsibilities and personal life? Insights from this question can guide improvements in work-life balance policies.

Action Steps to Enhance Employee Wellness

To address and support employee well-being, leaders can take these five proactive steps:

1. Implement Regular Wellness Check-ins: Schedule periodic one-on-one meetings with team members to discuss their well-being, workload, and any personal or professional concerns.

2. Provide Access to Mental Health Resources: Ensure employees have access to counseling services, mental health professionals, and stress management programs tailored to their needs.

3. Encourage Work-Life Balance: Promote flexible scheduling, adequate rest periods, and policies that support balancing work with personal life commitments.

4. Foster a Culture of Open Communication: Create an environment where team members feel safe to voice their concerns and know that their well-being is a priority.

5. Offer Continuous Training and Development: Provide opportunities for professional growth, resilience training, and skill development to help employees manage stress and improve their job satisfaction.

Conclusion

Investing in employee wellness is not just about supporting individuals; it enhances the overall effectiveness of organizations in high-stress professions. By prioritizing comprehensive wellness programs, resilience training, and fostering a supportive culture, we can ensure our teams are well-equipped to meet the challenges of their professions. As we continue to grow and learn in our leadership roles, let's remember that the well-being of our employees plays a significant part in the success and sustainability of our organizations.

5 Actionable Steps to Challenge Your Limits as a Leader

Embracing True Self

In leadership, the pressure to conform to expectations or portray a certain image can be immense. However, true leadership stems from authenticity—embracing who we are, with all our strengths and weaknesses.

We also need to avoid the "Me" "My" "I" trap. I have been working with a leader that has a hard time eliminating these self-serving words when referring to the team. It is easy to say "my team" or "I only hire the best" and especially the idea that "Come to me, I will fix the team and hold them accountable"

So, how do we avoid these and focus on the foundation for leadership?

Here is the stance we can take:

- **Patrons, Partners, Platform:** We should make no apologies for who we are. Valuing relationships and the platforms we use to share our voice is crucial.

- **Authenticity:** There is no need to pretend to be someone we are not. Embracing our true selves is key to genuine leadership.

- **Resilience:** Our past experiences, with all their scars, contribute to our ongoing learning and growth.

- **Integrity:** Standing for values and authenticity is vital. Being true to ourselves and our principles builds trust and respect.

- **Wisdom with Age:** As we grow older, it becomes clear that worrying about those who don't understand or appreciate our values is a waste of time.

Lessons in Leadership from Early Experiences

Reflecting on past experiences can offer invaluable lessons that shape leadership styles:

Every Little Action Matters

- Lesson Learned: In early jobs, like working at a family-owned retail garden center, every action impacts the business and its reputation.

- Application: As leaders, understanding that our actions set the tone for our teams and influence the broader organization is essential.

- Lesson Learned: Thriving leaders listen to staff and adapt to their interests, never relying solely on past successes.

- Application: Effective leaders stay attuned to changes in the team and with team members and pivot strategies to meet evolving needs.

Fostering a Supportive Team Culture

- Lesson Learned: Regular team get-togethers, from summer BBQs to winter events, foster strong, supportive cultures.

- Application: Building a cohesive and motivated team requires intentional efforts to create a positive and inclusive work environment.

The Power of Bearing in Leadership

Bearing—a leader's demeanor, composure, and presence—has a profound impact:

- Command Presence: Bearing is a cornerstone of discipline and professionalism, reflecting confidence and respect.
- Navigating Challenges with Grace: Bearing embodies authority and competence, inspiring resilience, and determination in teams.

Cultivating Mental Awareness and Confidence

To lead effectively, mental awareness and confidence are crucial. Here are strategies to enhance these qualities:

Mindfulness Practice

Dedicate time each day to mindfulness exercises such as deep breathing or meditation to enhance self-awareness and emotional regulation.

Communication Skills Development

- Invest in professional development opportunities to improve verbal and nonverbal communication, conveying confidence and empathy effectively.

Seek Mentorship

- Engage with mentors or personal coaches who can provide valuable feedback and guidance on enhancing leadership presence.

Embracing Leadership Risks: Visionary Leadership

True leadership involves taking chances and embracing the unknown:

- Visionary Leadership: Dare to dream big and think creatively. Inspire teams to achieve extraordinary results.
- Cultivating Innovation: Foster a culture where experimentation is encouraged, and failure is seen as a path to success.
- Courageous Decision-Making: Cultivate the courage to make tough decisions and trust instincts.

Expanding the Comfort Zone: 5 Actionable Steps

1. Change Perspective: Challenge yourself to see things from different angles, try brushing your teeth with the other hand.
2. Explore New Interests: Step outside comfort zones with new hobbies or interests, try something that you are afraid of trying.
3. Seek Feedback and Embrace Criticism: Invite constructive feedback from all levels and use it to grow.
4. Take Calculated Risks: Embrace opportunities to step look at the long term gain from a short term challenge.
5. Practice Resilience: Reframe challenges as opportunities for learning and growth.

Self-Evaluation Steps for Bearing

1. Observation and Feedback: Observe behaviors and seek feedback.

2. Reflection and Self-Assessment: Regularly reflect on actions and decisions.

3. Setting Clear Standards and Goals: Define specific behaviors and set measurable goals for improvement.

Commit to practices that enhance mental awareness and build confidence.

Lessons From a 15-Year-Old

As spring approaches, people rush to their local big-box retailers, eager to kickstart their gardening projects. Reflecting on my own experience many, many years ago, I remember working at a family-owned retail garden center as a 15-year-old kid, long before big-box stores became common. The lessons I learned there have profoundly shaped my approach to leadership.

Three Actionable Tips for Leaders:

1. Set Clear, Achievable Goals Break down your larger objectives into manageable steps. This not only makes it easier to manage cut the process also allows for regular celebrations of progress, reinforcing positive behavior. Establish a clear vision and mission for yourself, much like guiding your team. Invite feedback and contributions from trusted colleagues to shape your personal leadership journey.

Lesson from the Garden Center: One key lesson from my garden center days was the importance of clear, achievable goals. Dennis, one of the owners, always stressed that every little action matters. This came into play when I was caught flirting with the daughter of a customer (I was only 15 after all). Dennis explained that our actions reflect on the entire business. By setting clear, achievable goals, I learned to focus my energy on tasks that positively impacted the business.

2. Consistency is Key: Dedicate specific times each day to your new habits. Whether it is evening meditation after a long day, a daily reading session, or a morning workout (easy to get it in when you never know what the end of the day will be like) consistency helps reinforce your new routine and turns actions into habits. Embrace the discipline and structure you have experienced in diverse settings, from law enforcement to the military, to create a stable routine that fosters growth.

Lesson from the Garden Center: At the garden center, consistency was crucial. We had regular tasks and routines, from watering plants to stocking shelves. This consistency ensured that everything ran smoothly and taught me the importance of reliable habits. The owners also emphasized adaptability by listening to customers and evolving with their interests, ensuring the business's success despite market changes.

3. Embrace Accountability Share your goals with a coach like me, or trusted friend. Regular check-ins can provide the support and motivation needed to stay on track and adjust strategies as needed. Look for a coach who can help guide and challenge you to think critically, not just someone who answers questions for you, but helps you find the answer yourself. Evaluate the source of your feedback to ensure its constructive and reliable and ask open-ended questions to challenge areas are not spending much time on for improvement.

Lesson from the Garden Center: The owners of the garden center were great at holding us accountable while also supporting our growth. They fostered a positive work environment through regular company get-togethers, such as summer BBQs and winter gatherings. These events not only strengthened team bonds but also provided opportunities for mentorship and feedback.

Reflecting on Mental Focus and Confidence Building

Drawing inspiration from diverse experiences in law enforcement, the military, and the private sector, I have learned that mental focus and confidence are critical to effective leadership. Key skills to develop include:

- Effective Communication: Foster open, honest, and transparent communication within your team.

- Empathy and Compassion: Understand and support your team members to build strong, cohesive teams.

- Problem-Solving: Navigate complex issues within your organization with adept problem-solving skills.

Lesson from the Garden Center: Working at the garden center taught me the value of effective communication and empathy. The owners listened to what the customers were interested in and adapted their offerings accordingly. This customer-focused approach ensured their continued success and demonstrated the importance of empathy and adaptability in leadership.

Building a Positive Team Culture

Regular Company Get-Togethers The owners fostered a positive and inclusive work environment through regular company get-togethers. During the summer, we enjoyed BBQs at a local park, complete with volleyball games, all paid for by the owners. In the winter months, they hosted gatherings at their home or took the staff to Broncos games in Denver, using their season tickets. These activities not only strengthened team bonds but also showed the owners' appreciation for their staff's hard work.

Supporting Staff During Tough Times The owners' commitment to their employees extended beyond celebrations. They helped staff with expenses during the lean months of January and February when the garden center was closed before the spring rush. This support demonstrated their genuine care for their employees' well-being and fostered loyalty and dedication within the team.

Mental Conditioning for Leaders

Effective leadership begins with mental conditioning. Here are some techniques you can use to strengthen your mental focus and build confidence:

- Visualization Techniques: Regularly visualize your goals and the steps you need to achieve them. This practice can enhance your focus and prepare you mentally for success.

- Mindfulness Practices: Incorporate mindfulness exercises such as meditation and deep-breathing techniques to maintain mental clarity and reduce stress.

- Positive Affirmations: Use positive affirmations to build self-confidence and reinforce your belief in your leadership abilities.

Confidence Building Strategies

Building confidence is crucial for effective leadership. Consider these strategies:

- Reflect on Past Successes: Regularly remind yourself of your achievements and the challenges you have overcome. This reflection can boost your confidence in handling future obstacles.

- Continuous Learning: Stay committed to personal and professional growth by seeking new learning opportunities to get you outside of your comfort zone. This commitment demonstrates your adaptability and enhances your skill set.

- Constructive Feedback: Actively seek and embrace feedback from a coach, peers and mentors. Constructive criticism can help you identify areas for improvement and reinforce your strengths.

Challenge:

I challenge you to making a commitment for the next month, make it a daily practice to apply some of the concepts in this newsletter that will help support your goal of enhancing mental focus and building confidence. Share your progress and any obstacles you face in the comments.

3 by 4 Techniques to Help Transform Your Leadership Mindset

Are you ready to supercharge your mindset and build habits that stick? Let us discuss this process and look at how you can create a foundation for lasting personal and professional growth, enhancing your mental focus and confidence as a leader.

Three Actionable Tips for Leaders:

1. Set Clear, Achievable Goals Break down your larger objectives into manageable steps. This not only makes the process less daunting but also allows for regular celebrations of progress, reinforcing positive behavior. Establish a clear vision and mission for yourself, much like guiding your team. Invite feedback and contributions from trusted colleagues to shape your personal leadership journey.

2. Consistency is Key Dedicate specific times each day to building new habits while strengthening the current habits that have a positive impact on who you are as a leader. Whether it is morning meditation or workout or a daily time for reading (I enjoy this as a means to let go of the daily events), or an evening walk, consistency helps reinforce your new routine and turns actions into habits. Embrace the discipline and structure you have experienced in other settings, for me it runs from

law enforcement to the military, to create a stable routine that fosters growth.

3. Embrace Accountability Share your goals with a trusted colleague or mentor, have an accountability partner or coach like me. Regular check-ins can provide the support and motivation needed to stay on track and adjust as needed. Look for a coach who can guide with open ended questions and challenges you to get outside of your comfort zone, not just someone who gives you answers and solutions to issues instead of helping you find the answers. Evaluate the source of your feedback to ensure it is constructive and reliable, and be willing to ask the tough questions that look deeper into areas for improvement.

Reflecting on Mental Focus and Confidence Building

Drawing inspiration from diverse experiences in law enforcement, the military, and the private sector, I have learned that mental focus and confidence are critical to effective leadership. Key skills to develop include:

- Effective Communication: Foster open, honest, and transparent communication within your team.

- Empathy and Compassion: Understand and support your team members to build strong, cohesive teams.

- Problem-Solving: Navigate complex issues within your organization with adept problem-solving skills.

Mental Conditioning for Leaders

Effective leadership begins with mental conditioning. Here are techniques you can use to strengthen your mental focus and build confidence:

- Visualization Techniques: Regularly visualize your goals and the steps you need to achieve them. This practice can enhance your focus and prepare you mentally for success.

- Mindfulness Practices: Incorporate mindfulness exercises such as meditation and deep-breathing techniques to maintain mental clarity and reduce stress.

- Positive Affirmations: Use positive affirmations to build self-confidence and reinforce your belief in your leadership abilities.

Confidence Building Strategies

Building confidence is crucial for effective leadership. Consider these strategies:

- Reflect on Past Successes: Regularly remind yourself of your achievements and the challenges you have overcome. This reflection can boost your confidence in handling future obstacles.

- Continuous Learning: Stay committed to personal and professional growth by seeking new learning opportunities. This commitment demonstrates your adaptability and enhances your skill set.

- Constructive Feedback: Actively seek and embrace feedback from peers and mentors. Constructive criticism can help you identify areas for improvement and reinforce your strengths.

Call to action:

Commit to a daily practice that supports your goal of enhancing mental focus and building confidence. Share your progress and any obstacles you face with a peer or coach.

Unlocking Leadership Excellence: 5 Steps to Embrace the Power of Bearing

In the demanding duties of leadership, where challenges are constant and uncertainties common, one often-overlooked quality stands out: BEARING. Like a sturdy pillar that sets the foundation for a building, a leader's bearing supports the team, giving them support with poise and resilience through the demands of change.

Understanding Bearing in Leadership

Bearing encompasses more than mere physical posture; it is an embodiment of demeanor, composure, and presence. It reflects a leader's ability to maintain calm and confidence in the face of adversity, inspire trust and respect among team members. A strong bearing serves as a beacon of stability, fostering an environment where individuals feel secure and empowered to navigate challenges with courage and determination.

Bearing as a Command Presence

In the military, bearing is a cornerstone of discipline and professionalism. Marines are meticulously trained to maintain a strong bearing, radiating confidence, alertness, and respect in every interaction. From the crispness of their uniform to the precision of their movements, their bearing communicates a steadfast commitment to duty and honor. Similarly, in the corporate realm, bearing translates to maintaining a professional demeanor characterized by confidence, integrity, and grace under pressure. Imagine a business executive striding into a boardroom with unwavering confidence, commanding attention and respect with every word spoken, just like a Marine in full Dress Blues. Walk with confidence and stand tall.

Navigating Challenges with Grace

At its core, bearing embodies a command presence that transcends words, instilling confidence, and reassurance in those under its influence. A leader's bearing communicates authority and competence, serving as a guiding light in times of uncertainty. Whether delivering a critical briefing or navigating a high-stakes negotiation, a leader's bearing sets the tone for the entire team, inspiring them to rise to the occasion and achieve remarkable outcomes.

Cultivating Bearing for Lasting Impact

To cultivate bearing, leaders must embark on a journey of self-discovery and growth, prioritizing self-awareness, and emotional intelligence. By understanding their own strengths, weaknesses, and triggers, leaders can better regulate their responses and lead with clarity and conviction.

Embracing Self-Reflection

Self-reflection lies at the heart of bearing, offering leaders a mirror through which to examine their thoughts, actions, and intentions. Through introspection, leaders gain invaluable insights into their leadership style, enabling them to make informed decisions and course corrections as needed.

Take a moment to evaluate your own BEARING.

1. Observation and Feedback: Leaders can start by observing their own behaviors and interactions in various professional settings, such as meetings, presentations, or one-on-one conversations. They should pay attention to their posture, tone of voice, facial expressions, and overall demeanor. Seeking feedback from trusted colleagues, mentors, or executive coaches can also provide valuable insights into how their bearing is perceived by others.

2. Reflection and Self-Assessment: Taking time for introspection and self-assessment is crucial for evaluating one's bearing as a leader. Leaders can set aside regular periods for reflection, perhaps at the end of each day or week, to review their actions, decisions, and communication styles. They can ask themselves questions such as, "Did I maintain composure during challenging situations?" or "How did my demeanor impact the team's morale?" Honest self-assessment allows leaders to identify areas for improvement and refine their bearing over time.

3. Setting Clear Standards and Goals: Establishing clear standards and goals related to bearing can provide leaders with benchmarks for evaluation. Leaders can define specific behaviors or traits they aspire to embody, such as confidence, empathy, and professionalism, and set measurable goals for improvement. Regularly reviewing progress against these standards and goals enables leaders to track their development and adjust their approach as needed to enhance their bearing.

By incorporating these self-evaluation steps into their leadership practice, leaders can gain deeper insights into their bearing and take appropriate steps to refine and strengthen their command presence.

Action Steps to Improve Bearing:

1. Mindfulness Practice: Dedicate time each day to stop and take a mental break from the daily activity for mindfulness exercises such as deep breathing or meditation to enhance self-awareness and emotional regulation.

2. Communication Skills Development: Invest in professional development opportunities focused on enhancing verbal and nonverbal communication skills to convey confidence, empathy, and authority effectively.

3. Seek Mentor: Engage with mentors or executive coaches who can provide valuable feedback and guidance on enhancing your bearing and leadership presence.

4. Lead by Example: Demonstrate the behaviors and attitudes you wish to instill in your team, modeling resilience, integrity, and professionalism in all your interactions.

5. Celebrate Progress: Recognize and celebrate your growth journey, acknowledging the strides you've made while remaining open to continuous improvement.

As we continue to navigate the complexities of leadership, let us heed the wisdom of bearing, embracing its transformative power to inspire, guide, and lead with unwavering resolve.

Fostering Fairness and Recognition: 7 Principles to Help Elevate Your Leadership Through Praise

In our everyday duties of leadership, the thread of fairness and recognition weaves a pattern of trust and collaboration. As leaders, it is essential to extend the principles of praise not only within our professional realms but also across various areas of our lives.

Beyond the walls of our work environment, the concept of praise runs through our personal lives, family dynamics, communities, and social circles. It serves as a foundation for strengthening relationships, fostering camaraderie, and nurturing a sense of belonging.

Within our families, expressions of praise shape the bonds between parents and children, partners, and extended relatives. Acknowledging and celebrating achievements, both big and small, encourages a supportive environment where individuals feel valued and empowered to grow.

In our communities, acts of recognition amplify the spirit of unity and collective progress. Whether it is applauding the efforts of volunteers, honoring community leaders, or highlighting the accomplishments of local initiatives, praise fosters a culture of goodwill and collaboration.

Similarly, within our social groups, praise serves as a glue that binds friendships and fosters a sense of appreciation. By celebrating each other's successes, offering words of encouragement during challenges, and expressing gratitude for shared experiences, we create a nurturing environment that uplifts everyone.

The way we navigate these personal circles significantly influences our leadership style in professional settings.

Leaders who embrace the principles of praise in their personal lives bring a genuine spirit of appreciation and recognition to their teams. They understand the power of recognition in motivating and inspiring others, fostering a culture of trust and engagement.

We need to pay close attention to the praise or interaction we have with others.

As people, we tend to recognize those we associate with or those like-minded people we identify with. At times, this leads to more praise and interaction than we show others. A leader must be fair across the board. Find reasons to interact with others.

Here are five steps for self-reflection to ensure fairness in leadership:

- Assess Your Interactions: Take time to review your recent interactions with team members. Are there individuals you consistently engage with more than others?

- Evaluate Your Recognition Practices: Reflect on how you acknowledge the contributions of your team. Are there patterns of favoritism in your recognition efforts?

- Seek Feedback: Solicit feedback from your team members about your leadership style and recognition practices. Their insights can provide valuable perspective.

- Challenge Biases: Be mindful of any biases that may influence your interactions and recognition. Challenge yourself to treat all team members equally.

- Commit to Improvement: Make a conscious effort to interact with and recognize every team member regularly. Set goals to enhance fairness and inclusivity in your leadership approach.

Take time to consider how you received praise in your own lives and the impact different interactions influenced who you are today, as a person and as a LEADER.

We are the product of our environment and carry all of the learned experiences throughout our lives with us, directly impacting those we have the honor to lead.

Praise as a leader needs to be fair and spread out across the teams and organization we work in. Take a moment to consider the custodial staff or support staff that keep things rolling in your organization.

I recall a holiday, many years ago, where the team gave the administrative office staff a large gift basket to show appreciation for the work they do.

The problem came when our bureau chief came out of his office and picked out a piece of candy from the gift basket. I jokingly said they gift basket was intended for the staff who support the team not him. When you replied he does support the team, I said he is responsible for the team, the administrative staff take care of us. We both then thanked the staff sitting at their desks for the support they provide on a daily basis.

Praise needs to be serious and mean something, it can never be a token gesture or a way to check off a box on your to-do list as a leader.

Here are seven tools to build on your skills as a leader giving praise:

1. Regular Check-ins: Schedule regular one-on-one meetings with team members to provide personalized feedback and recognition.

2. Peer Recognition Programs: Implement peer recognition programs where team members can nominate their peers for outstanding contributions.

3. Public Acknowledgment: Celebrate achievements publicly through team meetings, newsletters, or social media platforms.

4. Thank-You Notes: Write personalized thank-you notes to team members to express appreciation for their efforts.

5. Skill-Building Workshops: Offer workshops or training sessions on effective communication and recognition techniques for leaders.

6. 360-Degree or upstream evaluations to provide Feedback: Gather feedback from peers, direct reports, and supervisors to gain a holistic view of your recognition practices.

7. Lead by Example: Demonstrate the value of recognition by consistently praising and appreciating the efforts of your team members.

By incorporating these self-reflection steps and utilizing these tools, we can create a culture of fairness and recognition that empowers every team member to thrive.

Embracing Patience: A Leader's Guide to Cultivating Trust and Clarity With Resilience

The Power of Patience in Leadership and Life

In the hustle and bustle of daily life, patience often feels like a scarce commodity. Yet, as leaders, we understand that patience is not only a virtue but a strategic imperative. Today, let us explore how embracing patience can not only transform our leadership approach but enrich our daily lives.

Embracing Patience in Leadership:

As leaders, we are tasked with guiding our teams and projects toward success. However, the rush to achieve results can sometimes take us off track and cause greater delays. Patience reminds us to pause, assess, and guide with intent. By taking the time to listen, observe, and understand, we foster a culture of collaboration and empowerment within our teams.

Guiding with Open-Ended Questions:

One powerful way to exercise patience in leadership is through the art of asking open-ended questions. Rather than rushing to provide solutions, invite dialogue and exploration by posing questions that encourage reflection and critical thinking. This approach not only empowers team members to contribute their unique perspectives but also fosters a sense of ownership and innovation.

Points to Consider When Tempted to Rush:

When faced with the temptation to rush a project or push our staff beyond their limits, we should consider the following:

1. Assess Realistic Timeframes: Take a step back and evaluate whether the timelines and expectations are realistic. Rushing a project can lead to compromised quality and burnout among team members.

2. Communicate Expectations Clearly: Ensure that your team understands the importance of patience and the reasons behind the project's timeline. Clear communication fosters understanding and buy-in, reducing the urge to rush.

3. Encourage Iterative Progress: Break down projects into manageable milestones and celebrate incremental progress. This approach not only keeps momentum high but also allows for course corrections along the way.

4. Practice Active Listening: When team members express concerns or challenges, practice active listening and empathy. Rushing past their concerns can lead to resentment and disengagement.

5. Lead by Example: As leaders, we set the tone for our teams. By modeling patience and resilience in the face of challenges, we inspire confidence and trust among our colleagues.

The Importance of Self-Reflection:

In our fast-paced world, the need for instant gratification often leads us to overlook the value of self-reflection. Yet, taking the time to pause and reflect on why we do what we do is essential for personal and professional growth. When we rush through life without stopping to reflect, we risk losing sight of our goals, values, and priorities. Self-reflection allows us to gain clarity, identify areas for improvement, and make more informed decisions.

Understanding the Urge to Rush:

Why do we feel the need to rush? In many cases, it stems from a fear of failure or a desire for control. We may worry that if we do not act quickly, we will miss out on opportunities or fall behind. However, rushing rarely leads to sustainable success. Instead, it often results in mistakes, stress, and dissatisfaction. By acknowledging our tendency to rush and practicing patience, we can break free from this cycle and lead with greater clarity and effectiveness.

Finding Balance in Patience:

Patience is not about feeling we are letting others down or complacency but about finding balance and perspective. It is about knowing when to act and when to wait, when to push forward and when to pause. As leaders, cultivating patience allows us to navigate challenges with grace and resilience, inspiring confidence, and trust in those we lead. So, let us embrace patience as a guiding principle in our leadership journey and as a source of fulfillment in our daily lives.

Unlocking Organizational Growth Through Leadership Exchange

In today's fast-paced landscape in any field, the concept of leadership exchange is gaining momentum as a strategic approach to foster organizational growth and cultivate dynamic leadership. As leaders, our impact extends beyond the confines of our current roles, presenting a unique opportunity to leverage our skills and experience to propel not just one, but multiple organizations toward success.

Embracing Change for Collective Growth: Leadership exchange involves leaders transitioning to new positions within or outside their current organization, with the aim of driving innovation, fostering collaboration, and nurturing talent across different areas of responsibility. This approach breaks traditional molds of leadership succession, offering a fresh perspective and injecting vitality into organizational culture. However, we as leaders should always look for those informal leaders within an organization that show the potential to lead others in a formal position.

Empowering Leaders to Flourish: By embracing leadership exchange, organizations empower leaders to explore new horizons, expand their skill sets, and embrace diverse perspectives. Such experiences not only foster personal and professional growth but also cultivate a culture of continuous learning and innovation within the broader ecosystem.

Maximizing Impact Through Collaboration: Collaboration lies at the heart of effective leadership exchange. By fostering partnerships between organizations, leaders can harness collective expertise, share best practices, and tackle complex challenges with agility and resilience. This collaborative spirit encourages us to build relationship where each party contributes to and benefits from the exchange of knowledge and insights.

Pioneering Change, One Leadership Exchange at a Time: As leaders, we possess the ability to shape the future of our organizations and industries. We need to look at the transformative power of leadership exchange, and step outside of our comfort zone to go beyond the familiar confines of our roles to explore new avenues of growth and innovation. Together, we can pave the way for a brighter, more interconnected future where leadership knows no bounds.

The Pitfalls of Job Hopping: While leadership exchange offers immense opportunities for growth, it is essential to recognize the negative impact of frequent job hopping. Continuously switching roles or organizations can undermine stability, hinder long-term strategic planning, and erode trust among team members. Moreover, it may impede the development of future leaders, as sustained commitment and investment in an organization are crucial for cultivating talent and fostering continuity.

Commitment to Organizational Development: To truly make a lasting impact and help organizations thrive, leaders must commit to serving an organization for a significant period, and not be constantly looking for the next opportunity. This commitment allows for the cultivation of deep-rooted relationships, the development of future leaders, and the implementation of sustainable strategies for long-term success. By investing time and effort into organizational development, leaders can leave a lasting legacy and create a positive ripple effect that extends far beyond their tenure.

Key Considerations for Leadership Transition:

1. Cultural Alignment: Ensure alignment between the leader's values and the organizational culture of the new role.

2. Stakeholder Engagement: Engage with key stakeholders to understand their expectations and build trust.

3. Skill Transferability: Identify transferable skills and experiences that can be leveraged in the new context.

4. Change Management: Develop a robust change management plan to navigate transition challenges effectively.

5. Continuous Learning: Embrace a growth mindset and commit to continuous learning to adapt to the new environment.

Action Steps for Successful Transition:

1. Self-Assessment: Reflect on personal strengths, weaknesses, and career aspirations to align with the new role.

2. Networking: Build relationships with peers, mentors, and industry experts to gain insights and support.

3. Training and Development: Invest in relevant training programs and development opportunities to enhance skills.

4. Communication: Communicate openly and transparently with stakeholders about the transition process and expectations.

5. Feedback Mechanism: Establish feedback mechanisms to solicit input and adjust strategies as needed to ensure a smooth transition.

Pause and Reflect: When facing the reality of change and growth, it is essential for leaders to pause and reflect on where we are, where we are going, and how we can best serve our organizations. Taking the time to assess our progress, recalibrate our strategies, and realign our priorities enables us to navigate challenges with clarity and purpose. As stewards of organizational success, let us lead with intentionality, empathy, and a steadfast commitment to excellence.

Mastering the Art of Leadership: Back Off, Reassess, and Redeploy

In the ever-changing landscape of leadership, we may need to take a strategic approach that involves stepping back, reassessing the situation, and redeploying resources effectively. This principle can be considered in a short statement as "back off, reassess, and redeploy," which is essential for navigating challenges and driving success in today's complex world.

As leaders, we are often faced with situations that require a thoughtful and measured response. By embracing the concept of stepping back, we afford ourselves the opportunity to gain perspective, evaluate the situation from different angles, and consider alternative approaches.

Reassessing involves a thorough examination of the current situation or challenge, identifying strengths, weaknesses, opportunities, and threats. It requires a willingness to challenge assumptions, seek input from diverse perspectives, and remain open to new ideas and insights.

Once we have gained clarity through reassessment, it is time to redeploy our resources strategically. This may involve reallocating personnel, adjusting priorities, or refining our strategies to better align with our objectives. This may also require us leaders to reconsider our approach to leading others. By leveraging our newfound insights and adaptability, we can optimize our approach and drive meaningful progress.

In my own leadership journey, I have found the "back off, reassess, and redeploy" approach to be invaluable. Whether navigating organizational challenges, leading teams through periods of change, or pursuing new opportunities, this strategic mindset has guided me towards success.

I have encountered numerous situations where the "back off, reassess, and redeploy" approach has been instrumental in overcoming obstacles and achieving success. For instance, when a team member failed to take action we had to consider if it was "training or conduct" and where we need to make adjustments to avoid it from happening again.

If we determine training was lacking, we need to step back and ask did we fail to train properly or was the training insufficient or outdated.

If we determine training was appropriate and the issue is conduct, we need to step back and assess if the issue was that the staff member did not care about the possible outcome or if leadership failed to provide adequate instruction or support.

These experiences show the importance of flexibility, adaptability, and a willingness to challenge conventional thinking. As leaders, we must recognize that our ability to back off, reassess, and redeploy is not only a reflection of our competence but also our commitment to fostering growth and innovation within our teams.

Key Points to Consider:

- Recognize when emotions are clouding judgment—a challenge for some leaders.

- Acknowledge when current strategies are not yielding desired results—a hurdle many leaders face.

- Pay attention to feedback from team members and stakeholders, which can be difficult for leaders accustomed to top-down decision-making.

Self-Reflection:

Effective self-reflection is essential in this process. Failure to step back and assess our own biases, assumptions, and emotional responses can cloud our judgment and impede our ability to make sound decisions. By cultivating self-awareness and regularly engaging in introspection, we can mitigate these obstacles and enhance our effectiveness as leaders.

Call to Action:

- Implement regular reflection sessions to evaluate current strategies.
- Foster a culture of open communication and feedback within your team.
- Encourage experimentation and innovation to discover new approaches.
- Seek mentorship or coaching to gain fresh perspectives on leadership challenges.
- Embrace continuous learning and personal development to enhance leadership skills.

As you navigate your own leadership journey, I invite you to explore how my coaching, training programs and presentation services can support your professional development. Whether you are seeking guidance on strategic decision-making, team building, or personal growth, I am here to provide personalized support and insights tailored to your unique needs.

Together, let us embrace the power of "back off, reassess, and redeploy" to unlock new opportunities, drive sustainable growth, and inspire positive change within ourselves and our organizations.

And, please share this with others that you feel might gain some insight on their own performance and growth to being an inspirational leader.

Nurturing Empathy: The Bedrock of Inspirational Leadership and Trust

In today's fast-paced world, empathy often takes a back seat in the pursuit of productivity and results. However, I have come to understand that empathy is not just a soft skill; it is part of the foundation for building trust, fostering stronger, more cohesive teams, and inspiring others to achieve the extraordinary. As someone who has traversed various roles—from law enforcement to leadership coaching—I have witnessed firsthand the transformative power of empathy in driving organizational success.

In this newsletter, I am thrilled to share insights and personal anecdotes that underscore the importance of empathy and inspirational leadership:

1. **The Human Element of Leadership:** Empathy is more than just understanding; it is about connecting with the human experience. I will share personal stories, such as taking the time to research celiac disease when an employee was diagnosed with it, or looking into the concept of "Zero-point energy" to support a team member's passion, despite my lack of understanding.

2. **Cultivating Trust and Understanding:** Through empathy, leaders can create environments where team members feel valued, respected, and understood. I encourage you to focus on practical strategies for

fostering empathy in the workplace, including active listening, seeking diverse perspectives, and showing vulnerability. Trust is the currency of leadership, and empathy is the foundation upon which it is built.

3. **Inspiring Through Empathy:** Inspirational leaders lead by example, demonstrating empathy in their actions and decisions. By understanding and empathizing with their team members' experiences, aspirations, and challenges, leaders can inspire them to reach new heights of performance and excellence.

4. **Case Studies in Empathy:** Drawing from my experiences and those of others, we will examine real-life examples of organizations that have embraced empathy and inspirational leadership, reaping the rewards of enhanced collaboration, innovation, and employee engagement. From small gestures of kindness to transformative cultural shifts, empathy has the power to ignite positive change.

5. **Q&A: Your Empathy Questions Answered:** Have questions about integrating empathy and inspirational leadership into your approach? Send them my way, and I'll address them in an upcoming Q&A session, offering personalized advice and insights tailored to your leadership journey.

By prioritizing empathy and inspirational leadership, we can create workplaces where compassion, understanding, and collaboration thrive. Together, let us embark on a journey of empathy-driven leadership that not only strengthens teams but also enriches lives and inspires greatness.

Seize the Opportunity: 5 Steps to Embrace Risk and Propel Your Growth

It is not just about managing the status quo but daring to envision and create what can be, not just standing on what is. Join us as we take up the profound journey of uncertainty and seizing opportunities to lead with innovation and courage.

Embracing the Unknown: As leaders, finding comfort in the familiar routine and operations is natural. Yet, true growth lies in our willingness to step into the unknown. It is about having the courage to take calculated risks and explore uncharted territories, even when the outcome is uncertain.

Visionary Leadership: At the core of taking chances is visionary leadership. It is about seeing beyond the present circumstances and envisioning a brighter future. By daring to dream big and think creatively, we inspire our teams to reach new heights and achieve extraordinary results.

Cultivating a Culture of Innovation: Innovation thrives in environments where leaders encourage experimentation and embrace failure as a path to success. By fostering a culture of innovation, we empower our teams to explore new ideas, challenge the status quo, and drive meaningful change.

Courageous Decision-Making: Taking chances demands courage – the courage to make tough decisions, confront adversity head-on, and persevere in uncertainty. As leaders, we must cultivate the courage to trust our instincts, follow our intuition, and lead with conviction.

Embracing Growth and Learning: Every chance we take is an opportunity for growth and learning. Whether we succeed or stumble, each experience shapes us into stronger, more resilient leaders. By embracing continuous learning and self-improvement, we turn every challenge into a stepping stone toward success.

Seizing Opportunities: In the ever-changing landscape of leadership, opportunities abound for those willing to take chances. Let us dare to dream, innovate, and lead with unwavering courage. Together, we can redefine what is possible and inspire others to do the same.

Expanding Your Comfort Zone: 5 Actionable Steps

1. Change Your Perspective: Challenge yourself to see things from a different angle. Whether it is sitting in a different chair during a meeting or rearranging your workspace, changing your physical perspective can open your mind to new possibilities and perspectives.

2. Explore New Interests: Step outside your comfort zone by exploring new hobbies or interests. Joining a new social group, trying out a new sport, or attending a workshop on a topic you know little about can expand your horizons and spark creativity.

3. Seek Feedback and Embrace Criticism: Invite feedback from colleagues, friends, and mentors, and be open to constructive

criticism. Embracing feedback, even when it is difficult to hear, can help you identify areas for growth and improvement.

4. Take Calculated Risks: Identify opportunities to step outside your comfort zone and take calculated risks. Whether it is volunteering for a new project at work or speaking up in a meeting with a bold idea, embracing risk-taking can lead to new opportunities for growth and success.

5. Practice Resilience: Building resilience is essential for navigating uncertainty and overcoming setbacks. Cultivate resilience by reframing challenges as opportunities for learning and growth, maintaining a positive mindset, and seeking support from your network when needed.

Unlocking Leadership Potential: Embrace the Leap in Faith!

In the dynamic landscape of leadership, there is a simple principle that often separates the good from the exceptional: the willingness to take a LEAP in faith. Leadership is not just about managing tasks; it is about navigating uncharted territories, facing tough challenges head-on, and inspiring others to rise to their best selves.

LEAP: Leadership in Action Leadership is not a stagnant role; it is a journey of continuous growth and learning. It requires the courage to step outside comfort zones, make difficult decisions, and embrace uncertainty with confidence. As leaders, we must be willing to take that LEAP of faith, trusting in our abilities and the abilities of the team combined with our vision to guide us through even the most challenging times.

"As I reflect on my four-decade-long journey in leadership, I'm reminded of the countless challenges, triumphs, and lessons learned along the way. From humble beginnings to navigating complex organizational landscapes, the path to leadership excellence has been marked by resilience, determination, and an unwavering commitment to growth."

Facing Tough Challenges Every leader faces different obstacles along the way – whether it is navigating organizational changes, managing conflicts, or steering through uncertain times. However, it is how we respond to these challenges that define our leadership journey. By embracing adversity as an opportunity for growth, we can inspire resilience, innovation, and positive change within our teams and organizations.

"Leaders need to be willing to let go of control of their staff, like holding putty in your hands, the harder you squeeze, the more putty you will have pushed out between your fingers."

Empowering Others True leadership is not about commanding from the top; it is about empowering others to unleash their full potential. By fostering a culture of trust, collaboration, and accountability, we create an environment where everyone feels valued and empowered to contribute their unique talents and perspectives. Together, we can achieve remarkable feats that surpass individual capabilities.

"Leadership requires a LEAP in faith, and the willingness to face tough challenges. It's about stepping into the role of a servant leader, dedicated to the growth, success, and well-being of each team member."

Inspiring the Extraordinary As leaders, our ultimate goal is not just to achieve the ordinary but to inspire others to reach the extraordinary. By setting a vision that challenges the status quo, encouraging innovation, and fostering a culture of continuous improvement, we empower our teams to surpass their own expectations and achieve greatness.

"Leadership is not about asserting authority or wielding power; it is about serving others and inspiring them to reach their full potential. As their Lieutenant, I am here to support and empower the team on every step of the journey to personal and professional growth."

5 Action Steps to Build Your Leadership Skills:

1. Continuous Learning: Commit to ongoing self-improvement through reading, training, and seeking mentorship opportunities.

2. Effective Communication: Practice active listening, clear articulation of ideas, and fostering open dialogue within your team.

3. Empathy and Emotional Intelligence: Cultivate empathy, understand others' perspectives, and manage emotions effectively in challenging situations.

4. Strategic Thinking: Develop strategic thinking abilities by analyzing problems critically, anticipating future trends, and formulating proactive solutions.

5. Lead by Example: Demonstrate integrity, resilience, and a commitment to ethical leadership in all your actions and decisions.

Join the Conversation I invite you to share your experiences and insights on leadership – what challenges have you faced, and how have you embraced the LEAP in faith to overcome them? Together, let us inspire and empower each other to reach new heights of leadership excellence and inspire others to achieve the extraordinary.

Unlocking Leadership Excellence: The Power of Developing, Not Controlling

In any leadership role, the ability to mold and develop staff is essential. Yet, I have seen to many leaders fall into the trap of attempting to exert control over others, only to find their efforts met with resistance and frustration.

So, let us explore the idea of nurturing, molding, and guiding staff instead of trying to control them.

Embracing the Role of a Mentor: Effective leadership begins with recognizing that our role is not to control, but to mentor and empower. Just as a sculptor shapes clay with care and precision, leaders mold and develop their staff, helping them realize their full potential. By fostering an environment of growth and learning, we empower our teams to thrive.

Building Trust Through Support: Trust is the foundation of any successful team. When leaders focus on developing their staff rather than controlling them, trust flourishes. By offering support, guidance, and encouragement, leaders create a culture where team members feel valued, respected, and empowered to excel.

Fostering a Culture of Collaboration: In a controlling environment, collaboration often takes a back seat to compliance. However, when leaders prioritize development over control, collaboration flourishes. By encouraging open communication, sharing knowledge, and diverse perspectives, leaders cultivate a culture where teamwork thrives and innovation flourishes.

Empowering Ownership and Accountability: True empowerment comes from allowing staff to take ownership of their work and decisions. Instead of micromanaging, leaders should empower their teams to make meaningful contributions and take calculated risks. By instilling a sense of accountability, leaders inspire ownership and drive results.

Adapting to Change and Growth: In today's fast-paced world, adaptability is key to success. Leaders who focus on developing their staff are better equipped to navigate change and uncertainty. By fostering a growth mindset and embracing continuous learning, leaders empower their teams to adapt, evolve, and thrive in any environment.

In conclusion, the path to effective leadership lies in the ability to develop and empower staff, rather than attempting to control them. Just as a gardener nurture and cultivates a garden, leaders nurture and develop their teams, fostering an environment where everyone can flourish.

Join me in embracing the power of development over control, and together, let us unlock the full potential of our teams.

"I Am Their Lieutenant, but They Are Not My Officers…"

Throughout my journey in leadership, spanning over four decades, I have come to understand that true leadership is about empowering and supporting those around you. It is about stepping into the role of a servant leader, dedicated to the growth, success, and well-being of each team member.

As their Lieutenant, my role is not to dictate or command, but rather to guide, mentor, and facilitate their individual and collective journey toward success. It is about creating an environment where each member feels valued, heard, and empowered to contribute their unique talents and perspectives.

In this newsletter, I would like to look deeper into the principles of servant leadership and how they can transform not only organizations but also individual lives. Let us explore how:

1. **Leading by Example:** Servant leadership starts with leading by example. By embodying the values and behaviors you wish to see in others, you set a standard of excellence and integrity for the entire team.

2. **Putting Others First:** A servant leader prioritizes the needs of their team members above their own. This means actively listening to their concerns, providing support and resources, and removing obstacles that may hinder their progress.

3. **Fostering Growth and Development:** One of the primary responsibilities of a servant leader is to foster the growth and development of their team members. This may involve providing opportunities for learning, offering constructive feedback, and recognizing and celebrating achievements.

4. **Building Trust and Collaboration:** Trust is the foundation of any successful team. As their Lieutenant, my goal is to cultivate a culture of trust and collaboration, where every member feels valued, respected, and supported.

5. **Embracing Diversity and Inclusion:** A servant leader recognizes the importance of diversity and inclusion in driving innovation and creativity. By embracing different perspectives and experiences, we can create a more inclusive and equitable workplace where everyone can thrive.

6. **Empowering Ownership:** Servant leadership involves empowering team members to take ownership of their work and decisions. By giving them autonomy and responsibility, we empower them to reach their full potential and contribute meaningfully to the team's success.

7. **Continuously Learning and Growing:** As their Lieutenant, I am committed to continuously learning and growing alongside the team. Together, we will navigate challenges, seize opportunities, and adapt to an ever-changing world with resilience and determination.

In conclusion, leadership is not about asserting authority or wielding power; it is about serving others and inspiring them to reach their full potential. As their Lieutenant, I am here to support and empower the team on every step of the journey to personal and professional growth.

Join me in embracing the principles of servant leadership and together, let us create a workplace where everyone feels valued, empowered, and inspired to excel.

Empowering Leadership With New Challenges

In today's demanding society, marked by uncertainty and change, it is imperative that leaders rise to the occasion and navigate challenges with resilience and resolve. As a Marine, leader in the private sector, retired law enforcement professional, and leader in school safety, I have witnessed firsthand the trials and tribulations that shape our society. Recent events have prompted me to share not just concerns, but also insights into fostering personal and professional growth amidst adversity.

The Role of an 'Indigo Warrior'

As an 'Indigo Warrior,' I stand firm in my commitment to a cause greater than myself. I am ready to offer support and assistance to others navigating the challenges of our current reality. Despite the passage of time, my dedication to empowering others on their leadership journey remains unwavering as they seek to be an inspirational leader.

Unveiling the Enigmatic World of Leadership

Indigo—a term laden with intrigue and mystery—evokes curiosity about its association with distinct personality traits, particularly within the realm of Indigo Children. Let us investigate this fascinating concept:

Indigo Children: Coined by "Nancy Ann Tappe," Indigo Children symbolize a shift in human evolution, possessing a profound spiritual awakening and a purpose beyond the ordinary. Their traits include:

- Spiritual Awakening: Deep connection to a higher spiritual realm.

- Confidence and Purpose: Emboldened by a larger mission.

- High Expectations: Holding themselves and others to high standards.

- Strong Intuition: Trusting innate intuition and skepticism of authority.

- Questioning Authority: Challenging established norms for peace and harmony.

Indigo Personality Traits: Beyond Indigo Children, traits associated with the indigo color include:

- Wisdom: Profound insight and understanding.
- Intuition: Strong intuitive abilities guiding decisions.
- Introspection: Reflective nature seeking deeper meaning.
- Spirituality: Drawn to spiritual pursuits for growth and enlightenment.

Unlocking Your Leadership Potential in Challenging Times

Embark on a journey with a comprehensive selection of keynote speeches, training sessions, and personalized coaching programs aimed at unlocking your leadership potential:

- **Exploring Leadership Skills:** Dig deep into effective leadership strategies through insightful speeches.

- **Training for Success:** Develop your leadership skills with tailored training programs covering communication, decision-making, team building, and conflict resolution.

- **Personalized Coaching:** Receive valuable insights and support from an experienced coach to unleash your full potential as a leader.

In times of uncertainty and adversity, the role of an 'Indigo Warrior' extends beyond personal growth—it encompasses supporting others through troubling times. As leaders, we stand together to inspire, empower, and develop those around us, fostering resilience and driving positive change in our organization and communities.

Challenges for Personal and Professional Growth

Amidst the challenges we face, embrace these opportunities for growth:

- Adaptability: Embrace change and adapt your leadership style to evolving circumstances. Ask your team for their input on new ideas and projects.

- Resilience: Overcome setbacks with resilience and determination, emerging stronger than before.

- Innovation: Foster a culture of innovation, seeking creative solutions to complex problems. Be willing to be "uncomfortable" try something new.

- Empathy: Cultivate empathy and compassion, understanding the diverse needs of those you lead. Take time to walk the floor and meet staff at their workstations.

- Continuous Learning: Commit to lifelong learning, staying informed and up to date with industry trends and best practices. Pick up a book on a topic you have not looked at previously.

Join us on this quest to unlock your leadership potential and make a lasting impact in your organization and beyond.

Disclaimer, Sources

This book contains references to military leadership principles, tactics, traits, and skills inspired by the Guidebook for Marines (Fourteenth Revised Edition, published by the Marine Corps Association, Quantico, Virginia, 1981) and the Handbook for Marine NCOs (United States Naval Institute, Annapolis, Maryland, 1979). These foundational works have played a vital role in shaping generations of Marine Corps leaders and serve as the cornerstone of my own leadership journey, beginning with my service in the United States Marine Corps.

The insights and leadership strategies presented throughout this book are drawn from my personal experience and the practical application of these principles, refined over decades of service in the military, law enforcement, and organizational leadership roles.

All interpretations, reflections, and applications of these concepts are solely those of the author and do not represent the official views or positions of the United States Marine Corps, the Department of Defense, the Marine Corps Association, or the United States Naval Institute.

This book is intended for educational and professional development purposes, applying timeless military leadership principles to contemporary leadership challenges in civilian and corporate environments.

If there is any inadvertent failure to credit a source that shares similar principles, materials, or references, please know that it is unintentional. I offer my sincere and personal apology for any misunderstanding or oversight that may arise as a result.

About the Author

Randall brings a wealth of life experiences to his role as an author, drawing from over 30 years of dedicated service in public safety and law enforcement. Having held positions such as Hostage Negotiations Sergeant and Critical Response Team Coordinator, his commitment extends beyond law enforcement, as he proudly served in the United States Marine Corps, embodying values of loyalty to God, country, Corps, family, and community.

However, Randall's journey is expansive, encompassing diverse roles in janitorial services, food plant production and sanitation, construction, academia, and sales. Holding a graduate degree in Organizational Leadership and Human Resources, Randall offers a solid foundation for evaluating organizational practices.

www.linkedin.com/in/randalldoizaki
https://www.doizakionleadershipllc.com